FORT MARTIN SCOTT

GUARDIAN OF THE TREATY

JOSEPH LUTHER

THE History PRESS

Published by The History Press
Charleston, SC 29403
www.historypress.net

Cover image: *Reveille at Fort Martin Scott*, Lee Casbeer, artist, by permission of Gillespie County Historical Society.

First published 2013

Manufactured in the United States

ISBN 978.1.60949.961.7

Library of Congress CIP data applied for.

Notice: The information in this book is true and complete to the best of our knowledge. It is offered without guarantee on the part of the author or The History Press. The author and The History Press disclaim all liability in connection with the use of this book.

To Norman and Marjorie Luther,
my adventurous parents.

Contents

Acknowledgements

My sincere appreciation for their kind consideration and cooperation is given to the following individuals and organizations that provided inspiration, information, critique and support for this research: Vicki Braglio Luther, Christen Thompson, Ryan Finn, Robert Claiborne, Evelyn Weinheimer, Bryant Saner, Tom Hester, Douglas Scott, Joe Davis, Jim McCrae, Jimmy Alexander, Leonard Bucsanyi, Lee Casbeer, Susan Dial, Deb Johnson, C.R. Caldwell, Randy Rupley, the Comanche National Museum and Cultural Center, the Hill Country Archaeological Association, the Texas Archaeological Association, the Fort Martin Scott Museum Association, the Gillespie County Historical Society, the Former Texas Ranger Foundation, the City of Fredericksburg, the Library of Congress, the National Archives, the Dolph Briscoe Center for American History, the Institute of Texan Cultures, the Texas State Library and Archives, the Texas State Historical Commission, the Texas Historical Society and Texas Beyond History.

INTRODUCTION

A cloud is a promise—rain is fulfillment.

–old proverb

The story of Fort Martin Scott in Texas can only be appreciated in the context of the convergence of the diverse influences that came into focus on this location in the mid-nineteenth century. Each of these externalities has its own distinct story, but together they created a synergy that is greater than the sum of the whole. This book is the story of how these disparate entities became a whole, each an essential element of the creation and life of Fort Martin Scott up to the present day.

Fort Martin Scott exists today because of the Pinta Trail, which was created by the aboriginal Indians more than ten thousand years ago. Eventually, these indigenous peoples were supplanted by invading Lipan Apache and Penateka Comanche bands who came to call this Hill Country home. Using this trail, the Spanish attempted to establish missions as early as 1684 to subdue the various tribes and bands. The Spanish missionaries and soldiers created the Presidio San Luis de las Amarillas and the nearby Santa Cruz de San Sabá Mission. There the Spanish, using Indian folklore, discovered the fabled Los Almagres silver mines, which continue to attract fortune seekers even today. James Bowie traveled this trail in search of the lost mines.

As settlers began to move westward along the Pinta Trail and up the various watersheds, the Republic of Texas went to war against the hostile Indians. The Texas Rangers patrolled this region in the 1830s and 1840s. Battles were fought, and legends were created. When Texas became part of the United States, the

U.S. Army was given the responsibility for peacekeeping and humanitarian services for all peoples of the Hill Country. Fort Martin Scott was the result.

The Adelsverein (German immigrants) came to this area full of promise and hope. They signed a lasting treaty with the Penateka Comanches, and the troops at Fort Martin Scott were given the responsibility, but not the authority, to safeguard this treaty.

The Treaty of Peace between John Meusebach and the Penateka band negotiated in March 1847 opened up almost four million acres for settlement. All or part of Concho, Kimble, Llano, Mason, McCulloch, Menard, San Sabá, Schleicher, Sutton and Tom Green Counties were created as a result of the treaty.[1] On May 9, 1847, the Comanche chiefs ceremoniously paraded into Fredericksburg to formally sign the Meusebach-Comanche Treaty at the Marketplatz.[2] This treaty was one of the most important pioneer works of the Germans in Texas. It allowed Meusebach's settlers to go unharmed into Penateka Comanche territory and the Penatekas to go to the white settlements; it also promised mutual reports on wrongdoing and provided for survey of lands in the San Sabá area, with a payment of at least $1,000 to the Indians. The treaty opened more than three million acres of land to settlement. It is believed to be the only Texas treaty made with the Indians that was not broken by either side. An annual "powwow" celebration has been held in Fredericksburg in honor of this unbroken treaty for many years.[3]

Fort Martin Scott was founded in December 1848 two miles east of Fredericksburg on Barons Creek. This army post was located on the site of Camp Houston, a locale developed in 1845.[4] The next year, the army named the post Fort Martin Scott in honor of a U.S. army officer killed in the war with Mexico. From 1848 to 1866, this post was staffed by the First U.S. Infantry, the Eighth Infantry, the Second U.S. Dragoons and the Fourth U.S. Cavalry, as well as various Texas Ranger companies, Confederate forces and home guard/militia units.

One may wonder why Fort Martin Scott was the first frontier fort in Texas. Was it created in fulfillment of the treaty? Was the fort sited here because of Pinta Trail and the Lost San Sabá mines? Was it built to protect United States interests from the Mainzer Adelsverein plans to create a German empire in Texas? Was it located here because it was on the threshold of Comancheria?

This is the first book devoted to Fort Martin Scott. This fact is remarkable given that this historic military post at Fredericksburg, Texas, is on the National Register of Historic Places[5] and has a recorded Texas Historic Marker.[6] The ruins also form a Texas State Archaeological Landmark.[7]

Reveille at Fort Martin Scott. Lee Casbeer, artist, by permission of Gillespie County Historical Society.

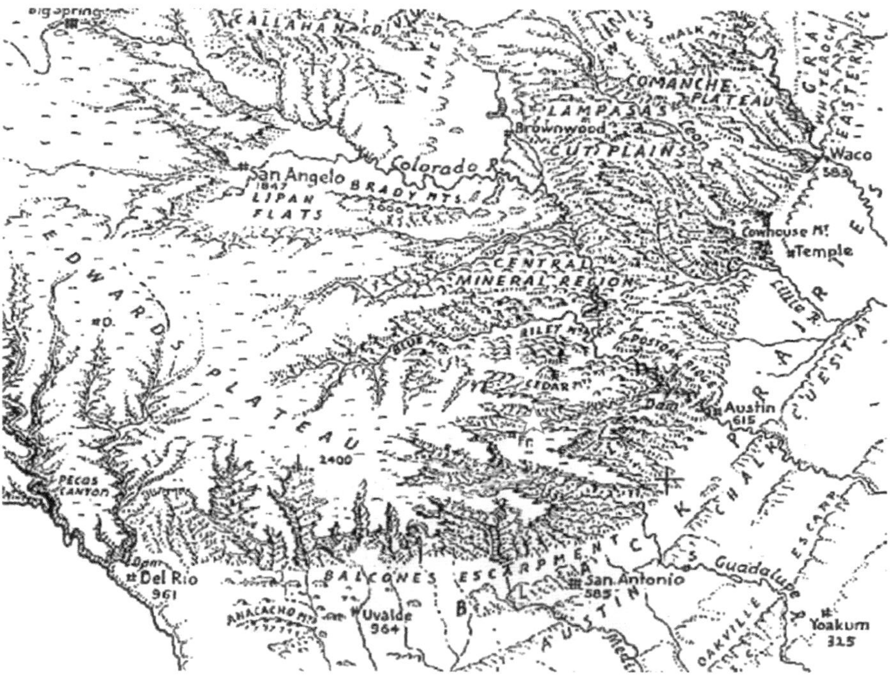

Location of Fort Martin Scott. *Adapted by permission from* Physiographic Map of the United States, *drawn by Erwin Raisz, 1957.*

Chapter 1
Pinta Trail

A great country for men and dogs, but hell on women and horses.
—old Texas proverb

Fredericksburg and Fort Martin Scott were established on the Pinta Trail.[8] This ancient trail appears to be the catalyst for the creation of this military post. Dating to the Paleo-Indian[9] times, the Pinta Trail was extensively used during the Forty-Niner gold rush and western migrations of the 1840s and later. More than three thousand "argonauts"[10] left from Texas in 1849. The route became widely known as the "Upper Emigrant Trail."[11]

Historically, the Pinta Trail linked San Antonio de Valero and the Spanish colonial presidio popularly known as San Sabá in present-day Menard County. From the city, early settlers trailed through the pass at Leon Creek (29° 39' 56" N, 98° 37' 37" W), historically known as La Puerta (de las Casas) Viejas (roughly translated as "gateway to the old houses," or "old pass"). The pass and the immediate vicinity of the Pavo Real archaeological site[12] became a documented Comanche trail leading northward from the San Pedro Springs in San Antonio. In the early history of the Béxar settlement, the historical trail also may have been called the Camino de Tehuacanas (an apparent reference to the Tawakonis, a Wichita group commonly associated with north-central Texas throughout the eighteenth century).[13]

The Pinta Trail, which extended about 180 miles northwest from San Antonio to the site of Presidio San Luis de las Amarillas and nearby Santa Cruz de San Sabá Mission near Menard,[14] has served as a transportation

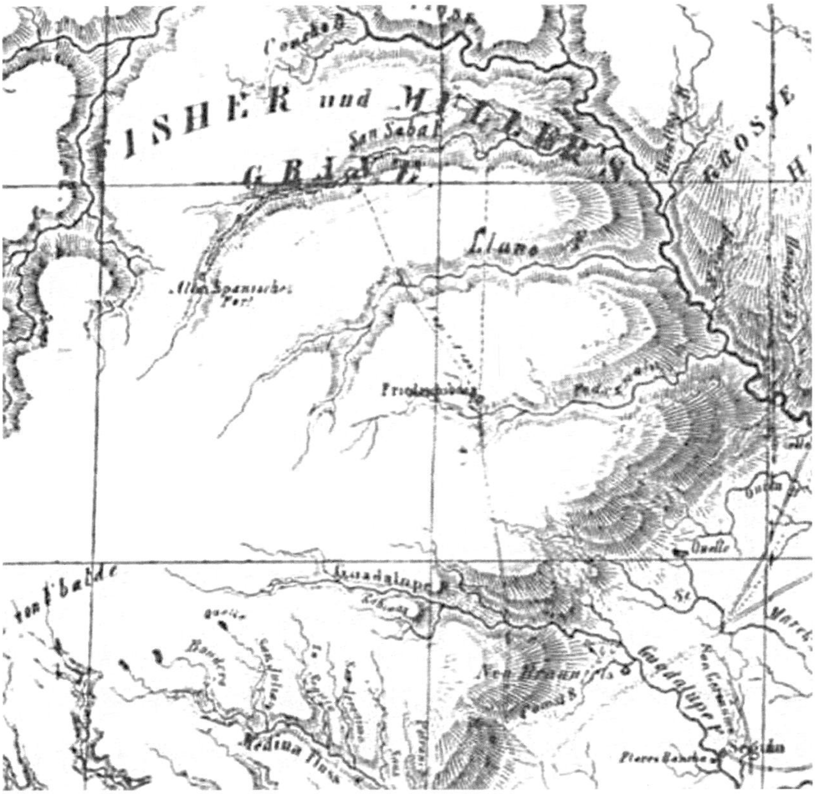

Pinta Trail. *Karte des Staates Texas aufgenommen in die Union 1846: nach der neuesten Eintheilung*, 1849. *Courtesy of University of Texas–Arlington Library.*

route through the Hill Country from the time of the prehistoric Indians (12,000 BP) to the present.

The Santa Cruz de San Sabá Mission and its Presidio San Luis de las Amarillas[15] were established in 1757 because of the Spanish mines known as Los Almagres.[16] It is a crucial fact that the fabled silver mines were the "ace in the hole" for the German Immigration Company. Dr. Ferdinand von Roemer[17] reported that "it was our intention from the very beginning to visit this fort, since there was a persistent rumor among the Texas settlers that the Spaniards had worked some silver mines in the vicinity of the fort."[18]

Prince Karl (or Carl) Solms-Braunfels[19] mentioned the Spanish mines in his book *Texas, 1844–1845*: "As to the knowledge of the mountains of the Fisher-Miller grant, most of it is obtained from the Mexicans, who in turn received it from the nomadic Indians. They describe the mountains as rich in ore, especially copper and silver."[20]

In 1849, the road from San Antonio ran through Fredericksburg to California. This route continued into the Comanche country beyond the Llano and into what is now Mason County. From the presidio, the trail divided, with one branch going to Fort McKavett and up to the head of the San Sabá near Sonora, where it turned west to the Pecos River. The other branch went northwest to the Concho River and eventually to Santa Fe.[21]

The Pinta Trail ran as straight as an arrow into the heart of Comancheria.

Chapter 2
Comancheria

They swept everyone off the Southern plains. They nearly exterminated the Apaches. They were warlike by nature. And you know, if you look at, say, the Comanches, and then you look back in history at, for example, you know, Goths or Vikings or Mongols or Celts—or old Celts are actually a very good parallel—in a lot of ways I think we're looking back at earlier versions of ourselves. We—we being white Europeans—did all of those things.[22]

–S.C. Gwynne

The Texas historian T.R. Fehrenbach wrote the following about the Comanches: the *Nermernuh* (the "True Human Beings," the Comanches) "destroyed the ancient dream of the Spanish empire in North America; they shredded the Mexican frontier; they blocked the French advance into the Southwest; and they delayed the advance of the Anglo-American conquest of the continent for almost sixty years."[23]

At the time Fort Martin Scott was established in 1847, it was the first frontier fort in Texas. It stood on the Pinta Trail at the gateway to the Comanche heartland—the greatest threat to the advancement of Texas civilization at that time. The Llano River was the threshold.

Comancheria is the name commonly given to the region of New Mexico, west Texas and nearby areas occupied by the Comanches. Before the Comanches expanded out of present-day Wyoming in the early eighteenth century, the region now known as Comancheria was home to a mixture of tribes, most notably the Apaches. Much of the territory had previously been known as Apachería.

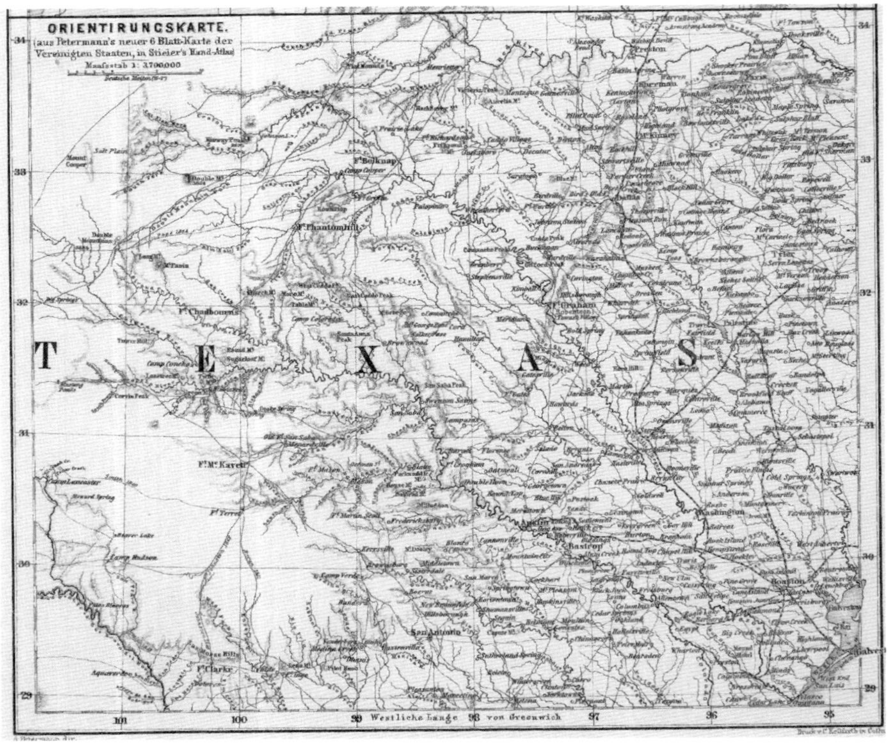

Orientirungskarte. Petermann, artist, in Stieler's Hand Atlas, *sixth edition (1871–75).*

The word "tribe" should be used with prudence in regard to the Comanches. Though they had a common language and way of life, Comanches had no political institutions or social mechanisms by which they acted as a unit. Comanche families formed bands that acted autonomously from one another. Bands have generally been delineated geographically—as "northern," "middle," "southern" and "Llano Estacado"—but Comanche bands did not really adhere to any distinct territorial boundaries. Furthermore, Comanche bands were not fixed institutions; they broke apart, reformed and merged over the years.[24]

The Comanche bands included the Penatekas (Honey-Eaters) in the southern Hill County, north of the Balcones Escarpment. The Wanderers, Wasps, Liver-Eaters and Buffalo-Eaters roamed to the north of the Penatekas. Even farther north in Texas were the Yap-Eaters. The Llano Estacado[25] itself was the domain of the Quahadi—the Antelope Band—perhaps the fiercest of the Comanches. This was Quanah Parker's band.[26]

The ancestors of the Texas Comanches were the historic Shoshones of California, Idaho, Nevada, Utah and Wyoming. They were of the Uto-Aztecan linguistic stock, a Native American language family consisting of more than thirty languages. The Comanche language and the Shoshone language are quite similar. The Comanches become apparent as a definite group shortly before 1700, when they broke off from the Shoshone people living along the Upper Platte River in Wyoming. This divergence coincided with their adoption of the horse.[27]

The horse was a fundamental ingredient in the manifestation of a distinctive Comanche culture. Some scholars have suggested that the Comanches broke away from the Shoshones and moved southward to search for additional sources of horses among the settlers of New Spain in New Mexico. The Comanches may have been the first group of Plains natives to fully incorporate the horse into their culture and to introduce the animal to the other Plains peoples.[28]

The horse also appears to be the basis of competition for resources carried out by the Comanches. David G. Burnet wrote in 1824, "As the Comanchees [*sic*] do not cultivate the ground, but derive their subsistence from the spontaneous productions of nature, and chiefly from the animal kingdom, they are necessarily migratory, and obliged to change their encampment every ten or fifteen days."[29] The Comanches fought the Apaches for horses and for water and pasture to sustain their horses.

The Comanches ranged in search of horses and sufficient grass and water to care for them. A particular locale could be quickly "grazed off" and rendered inadequate for pasturage. This circumstance was particularly critical due to the large number of horses possessed by the Comanches. Gerald Betty, in his book on Comanche society, wrote, "The daily maintenance of their animals probably encouraged the majority of their ambulations."[30]

Comanche raids were legendary for the distance covered, striking hundreds of miles from their starting points. So many raids took place by moonlight that a full, bright moon is still known as a "Comanche moon."[31]

In the Texas Hill Country, the Penateka band of Comanches was virtually unchallenged. So superior were these warriors that development west of the Balcones Escarpment came to a virtual halt. T.R. Fehrenbach, in his book on the Comanches, wrote about the "Comanche barrier," noting, "By 1750, few, if any, surrounding peoples dared set foot in Comanche country."[32]

Much has been written about the savagery of the Comanches. This was a clash of cultures as the Comanches fought by their own customs, radically different from the Euro-Americans. What appeared as hideous atrocities to the settlers was a cultural ritual by the Comanches. Fehrenbach wrote:

Comanche Camp. *Photo by William S. Soule, 1869–74.*

> *The Anglo-Americans shared a common Indo-European cultural consciousness. This heritage included concepts of private property, hierarchy and aristocracy, moral dualism, and forms of serfdom, slavery, or other subordination. On the other hand, the "Amerindians" were isolated from all Europeans by worldviews and cultural divergences that had been widening for at least four thousand years. To become "civilized" like the Anglo-Americans, the truly primitive tribesman had to do more than learn a new language or pick up a few new techniques. He had to betray his whole concept of the world and man's role in it. The Amerindian spirit world and the European universe of cause and effect did not just exist on higher and lower technical planes. They were utterly disparate and intimately hostile.*[33]

Pekka Hämäläinen substantiated that from the 1750s to the 1850s, the Comanches were the prevailing group in the Southwest, and the domain they ruled was known as Comancheria. Hämäläinen called it an empire. Confronted with Spanish, Mexican and American outposts on their periphery in New Mexico, Texas, Louisiana and Mexico, Comanches worked to enhance their own safety, prosperity and power.

The Comanches used their military supremacy to obtain goods and labor from the Americans, Mexicans and Indians through thievery, tribute and kidnappings. "Although powered by violence," Hämäläinen wrote, "the Comanche empire was primarily an economic construction, rooted in an extensive commercial network that facilitated long-distance trade." Dealing with subordinate Indians, the Comanches spread their language and culture across the region. Their empire collapsed when their villages were repeatedly decimated by epidemics of smallpox and cholera in the late 1840s; the population had plunged from twenty thousand to just a few thousand by the 1870s.[34]

Comanche Warriors

Warriors to the core, Comanches probably acquired their name from a Ute word meaning "anyone who wants to fight me all the time." Hunting and combat from horseback so engaged the Comanches that they seemed more at ease riding than on foot. The artist George Catlin observed, "In their movements they are heavy and ungraceful; and on their feet one of the most unattractive and slovenly races of Indians I have ever seen; but the moment they mount their horses, they seem at once metamorphosed, and surprise the spectator with the ease and grace of their movements." Mounted Comanche warriors were the most fearsome enemy ever faced by other Indians and Europeans alike in Texas.[35]

Catlin painted the Comanches in the summer of 1834. With his artist's eye for detail, he noted their horsemanship. "He drew the reins upon a heavy Spanish bit, and every jump, plunged into the animal's sides, till they were a gore of blood, a huge pair of spurs."[36] The Comanches had learned from the Spanish the equestrian skills necessary to maintain and enhance their use of the horse. They replicated the Spanish saddles, bits, spurs, lassos, corrals, lances, herd management and decoration.[37]

In the spring of 1836, the main movement of early Euro-Texas settlements was up the south-central river valleys of the Brazos, Colorado and Guadalupe. The Comanches fiercely resisted their encroachments with destructive and deadly raids on the frontier. Just above the Balcones Escarpment, where the Penateka Comanches liked to camp in the Hill Country canyons, the Texans and Comanches began to do battle.[38]

A cycle of raiding and retaliation on both sides climaxed during the presidency of Mirabeau B. Lamar. By July 25, 1839, the campaigns had destroyed or removed virtually all of the Native American population in the eastern half of Texas, opening up thousands of acres for settlement. The west was a different story. Despite campaigns by the Texas Rangers, the lands west of the Balcones Escarpment were in the control of the Penateka Comanches. Frontiersmen to the south and east of the Edwards Plateau continued to be in constant peril.[39]

The Comanches were a splendid and fearsome people. Billy Dixon, the buffalo hunter and frontier scout, described a Comanche charge at Adobe Walls:

> *There was never a more splendidly barbaric sight. In after years I was glad that I had seen it. Hundreds of warriors, the flower of the fighting men of the Southwestern Plains tribes, mounted upon their finest horses, armed with guns and lances, and carrying heavy shields of thick buffalo hide, were coming like the wind. Over all was splashed the rich colors of red, vermilion and ochre, on the bodies of men, on the bodies of running horses. Scalps dangled from bridles, gorgeous war-bonnets fluttered their plumes, bright feathers dangled from the tails and manes of the horses, and the bronzed, half-naked bodies of the riders glittered with ornaments of silver and brass. Behind this head-long charging host stretched the Plains, on whose horizon the rising sun was lifting its morning fires. The warriors seemed to emerge from this glorious background.*[40]

A Comanche, riding at gallop, could loose twenty arrows while a musket-armed soldier could only get off one shot before reloading. Metal arrowheads became popular in the late seventeenth century. Low-grade iron arrow points turned out in quantity by forges were greatly sought after. A trading house could supply a packet of one dozen arrow points to the Indians at a cost of one medio real (sixteenth of a Spanish dollar, half a bit or six cents). Over two centuries, these iron arrowheads killed more human beings of both races than all the guns traded to the Indians combined.[41]

A local captive of the Comanches, Clinton L. Smith, wrote in his book about his life as a warrior:

> *They made their arrows out of dogwood switches, and made their bows out of wild mulberry and bois d'arc. In slipping around through the white settlements the Indians would pick up all of the hoop iron they could find and use this in making their arrow spikes. They also traded for this kind*

> *of iron from the Mexicans. Many people have asked if we used stone arrow spikes. We knew nothing about this kind of an arrowhead, for they belonged to tribes of a former age. The Mexicans also brought in iron or steel arrow spikes ready made, and all we had to do was fit them on a dogwood shaft and sharpen them.*[42]

Mirabeau B. Lamar abandoned Sam Houston's peace efforts, which he considered a failure, in favor of waging all-out war on the Comanche nation. Lamar's policy culminated in the "Council House Fight" in Béxar County. By invitation, thirty-three Penateka chiefs and warriors, accompanied by thirty-two other Comanches, arrived in San Antonio on March 19, 1840. Texas soldiers entered the Council House,[43] where the peace talks were being held, and the commissioners informed the assembled chiefs that they were to be held as hostages until the remaining captives were released. In the ensuing melee, Texans attacked several Indians, while soldiers killed most of the Comanches who remained in the Council House courtyard. In the Council House Fight, thirty Penateka Comanche leaders and warriors, as well as some five women and children of the tribe, were killed by Texas troops in downtown San Antonio.[44]

Comanche loathing of Texans, who were regarded as mendacious, continued throughout the warfare era and contributed much to the viciousness on the frontier. In the summer of 1840, the Comanches swept down the Guadalupe Valley, killing settlers, stealing horses, plundering and burning settlements. More than five hundred warriors led by Buffalo Hump, the celebrated war chief of the Penateka Comanches, raided the towns of Victoria and Linnville, killing twenty-five Texans.

After the Linnville raid of 1840, the Comanches rode north, where they were intercepted on August 12, 1840, at Plum Creek near the site of present-day Lockhart.[45] The Comanches were routed by a volunteer army under General Felix Huston,[46] Colonel Edward Burleson and Captain Matthew Caldwell, as well as with Texas Rangers under Captain Ben McCulloch. Though some fifty Comanches were killed in the Battle of Plum Creek, the Texans continued to seek retribution. In October, Texas troops under the command of Colonel John H. Moore traveled three hundred miles up the Colorado River and destroyed a Comanche encampment near the site of present Colorado City.[47]

With entry into the Union, migration to Texas rose considerably. The state's population tripled between 1850 and 1860, the country west of San Antonio, Austin and Dallas filled up with settlers and the new army forts attracted settlements that sprang up near them. The influx of newcomers and the passing caravans of Forty-Niners on their way to the gold mines of California also brought a new wave of disease that laid waste to the Indians.

The Comanches were hit by smallpox in 1848 and cholera in 1849; by some estimates, half their population died.[48] Cholera was a fast killer. Its incubation period was from two hours to five days. More often, the time from the moment of infection to the death of a healthy adult Comanche male was only a matter of hours. "It is believed that half of the still surviving Penateka died."[49]

The buffalo population began declining during the same period. Partly, the expansion of white settlement and the federally sponsored "Indian removal" program that put fifty thousand eastern Indians on the margins of the South Plains reduced available buffalo range and increased the number of people hunting them. But the Indians' hunting practices also contributed to the diminishment of the buffalo. They preferred to hunt buffalo cows because their meat was more tender and their hides easier to process into finer robes. This overhunting of breeding-age females contributed to the falloff of the herds. Comanches took to eating their horses, and this depletion of their most important form of property provoked them to increase their cattle raids on both sides of the Rio Grande. Comanches also began to attack others who hunted the buffalo.[50]

Chapter 3
Penateka Comanches

Our great Father knows that I was the first Comanche who came to see Sam Houston, only to shake his hand in friendship, but I took him in my arms and told him my heart was his.
—Mo'pe-choko-pa (Old Owl), Penateka Comanche chief

Of all the bands of Comanches in Texas, it was the Penateka who posed the greatest threat to travelers on the Pinta Trail, German immigrants, the Texas Rangers and Fort Martin Scott. The Penateka (*Pen*-ah-took-uh), or "Honey-Eaters," band of Comanches occupied the Balcones Escarpment and especially the San Sabá River region. Their range extended from the Edwards Plateau to the headwaters of the central Texas rivers. Because of their site and situation, the Penatekas played the most legendary role in Texas history. "In legend and history, the Penateka were the largest and most powerful of all Comanche bands. They had swept the Apaches into Mexico and fought the Spanish to a standstill in Texas."[51]

Buffalo Hump (Po-che-na-qua-heip)

Buffalo Hump was the war chief and representative of the Penatekas, largest and most famous band of the Comanches.[52] In 1844, Buffalo Hump met

Modern Comanche warrior. Frederic Remington, artist.

with Sam Houston at Tehuacana Creek[53] and demanded that the white men stay off the Edwards Plateau, west of the Balcones Escarpment. In so doing, the Comanches were defining their frontier boundary as the Balcones Escarpment. President Houston tacitly agreed to this condition, and Texas Indian agents provided Buffalo Hump with gifts to demonstrate their goodwill. In spite of this, the Texas government was unable to hold back the surge of frontiersmen onto Comanche lands. Consequently, the Comanches resumed their raids. In response to these attacks, Texas Rangers assaulted Penateka encampments.[54] Although Buffalo Hump managed to continue to fight for some time, in May 1846, he led the Comanche delegation at Council Springs and signed a treaty with the United States.[55]

Ferdinand Roemer, a noted German scientist who was traveling in America at the time of the meetings in 1847, attended the Fredericksburg council between the chiefs and white representatives. Roemer characterized Buffalo Hump vividly as

> *the pure unadulterated picture of a North American Indian, who, unlike the rest of his tribe, scorned every form of European dress. His body naked, a buffalo robe around his loins, brass rings on his arms, a string of beads around his neck, and with his long, coarse black hair hanging down, he sat there with the serious facial expression of the North American Indian which seems to be apathetic to the European. He attracted our special attention because he had distinguished himself through great daring and bravery in expeditions against the Texas frontier, which he had engaged in times past.*

Buffalo Hump came to prominence after the Council House Fight[56] when he led the Comanches on the Great Raid of 1840.[57] Buffalo Hump was resurrected as a powerful historical figure by Larry McMurtry's books *Dead Man's Walk* and *Comanche Moon*, the first two books in the "Lonesome Dove" series. Whether intentionally or not, McMurtry's dramatization of the character of Buffalo Hump is very similar to the historical figure described so vividly by Roemer. Buffalo Hump is also mentioned in a scene in the film *The Outlaw Josey Wales* when Lone Watie tells Wales that he and Buffalo Hump were among a delegation that was sent to Washington, D.C., to meet with government officials during Lincoln's administration.[58]

As war chief of the Penateka Comanches, Buffalo Hump dealt peacefully with American officials throughout the late 1840s and 1850s. In 1849, he guided John S. Ford's expedition part of the way from San Antonio to El Paso, and in 1856, he sadly and finally led his people to the newly established

Comanche reservation on the Brazos River. Continuous raids from white horse thieves and squatters, coupled with his band's unhappiness over their lack of freedom and the poor food provided on the reservation, forced Buffalo Hump to move his band off the reservation in 1858. While camped in the Wichita Mountains, the Penateka band under Buffalo Hump was attacked by United States troops under the command of Major Earl van Dorn. Allegedly not aware that Buffalo Hump's band had recently signed a formal peace treaty with the United States at Fort Arbuckle, Van Dorn and his men killed eighty of the Comanches.

An aged and weary Buffalo Hump led and settled his remaining followers on the Kiowa-Comanche reservation near Fort Cobb in Indian Territory in Oklahoma. There, in spite of his enormous sadness over the end of the Comanches' traditional way of life, he asked for a house and farmland so that he could set an example for his people. Attempting to live out his life as a rancher and farmer, he died in 1870.[59]

SANTA ANNA (SANTANA)

Santa Anna (circa late 1790s–1849) was a Native American war chief of the Penateka band of the Comanche Indians. He was an important chief during the 1830s and 1840s, though probably less influential than Buffalo Hump. Santa Anna was a frequent visitor at Fort Martin Scott. He was the first member of his band to visit Washington, D.C. He was originally, along with Buffalo Hump, a leader of Comanche resistance to Anglo settlement in Texas, especially during the period following the Council House Fight. He was the father of Carne Muerto, later a war chief of the Quahadi band of Comanches. Before 1845, he was firmly identified with the militant faction of his tribe that opposed accommodation with whites. In point of fact, there is absolutely no record of his ever meeting with officials representing the government of the Republic of Texas. He appeared during this time to be even more militant than Buffalo Hump, who met with Sam Houston in 1843–44.[60]

In early December 1847, Santa Anna and a party of chiefs from several tribes in Texas visited Washington, D.C. The first of his tribe to make such a journey, Santa Anna was recorded to be overwhelmed by what he saw, especially the sheer numbers of the whites. From that moment on, convinced that continued armed resistance against the United States was tantamount to suicide for his people, he began advocating accommodation and attempted to use his prestige as a noted war chief to secure a lasting peace. But among the still warlike Comanches, Santa Anna's conversion reduced his prestige.[61]

Santa Anna apparently grew tired of his reduced position, and to regain his former glory, he led several raids into Mexico in 1848–49, violating the Treaty of Guadalupe Hidalgo. These raids necessitated intervention by the army and United States Indian agent Robert S. Neighbors, and Santa Anna was persuaded to stop. In late December 1849, a cholera epidemic killed more than three hundred Penateka Comanches in a few weeks' time. Santa Anna was one of the victims, although Buffalo Hump, who also took ill, survived. Following Santa Anna's death, the Penateka band, other than the division commanded by Buffalo Hump, disintegrated. Surviving members joined other Comanche bands.[62]

Old Owl (Mopechucope)

Old Owl was among the greatest of the Penateka civil (or peace) chiefs. Although known as a civil chief, he was also known to lead war parties. He was an important chief, though probably less influential than Buffalo Hump during the 1830s and 1840s. He was originally, along with Buffalo Hump and Santa Anna, a leader of Comanche resistance to Anglo settlement in Texas, especially during the period following the Council House Fight. Old Owl died during the epidemics of 1848–49. It is believed that, like Santa Anna, he died of cholera in 1849, but he may have died the previous year during the smallpox epidemic.[63]

Robert S. Neighbors recorded one of the best-known meetings with Old Owl. While he was a Texas Indian agent for the republic in 1845, Major Neighbors was at a Tonkawa camp. Old Owl arrived with forty warriors and, in a manner the major called "most insolent," demanded that the Tonkawas feed the war party and their horses and provide for them entertainment. The Tonkawas, in fear for their lives, provided forty women, food and shelter and cared for the horses at once. Neighbors, who had just been appointed Indian agent for all Texas Indians, including the Comanches, took this opportunity to meet some of his new charges and told them that he was hopeful of civilizing them. Old Owl, introduced to Neighbors, complimented him on his fine blue coat. Neighbors, understanding the meaning of this compliment, presented the chief with the coat immediately. Other warriors admired his pants, boots and other clothing, and soon Neighbors was standing only in a nightshirt.[64]

KATEMCY (CA-TUMSIE, KETEMOCZY)

Comanche chief Katemcy is one of the unrecognized champions of the Penateka Comanches. Although a subchief under Santa Anna, it was Katemcy who first met with Meusebach at Gamel Springs on February 5 at the present-day site of Mason. On February 7, the expedition visited Katemcy at his winter camp at Devil Spring (30° 54' 35" N, 99° 14' 56" W) and made arrangements for the meeting with Old Owl and Buffalo Hump at Sloan Springs on the San Sabá River.[65]

Writing in the *Frontier Times*, Leonard Passmore described Katemcy as "a very dignified old chief [who] was held in great admiration by all the members of his tribe." The winter camp of this Comanche chief was near the modern Texas village of Katemcy. The chief's name was also spelled as Ketemoczy by the Germans. Leonard Passmore also noted that "among the cliffs and deep little gorges of these granite rocks the old chief and his tribe would spend the winter, and then in the springtime move to more pleasant quarters down on the San Sabá, near the present village of Camp San Sabá."[66]

Today, the community of Katemcy is located on Farm to Market Road 1222, one mile east of Texas State Highway 87. The area was used for many years as pastureland by Comanche Indians, who periodically burned off the brush to encourage the growth of the prairie grass. Today, this area is a park and a recreational area called Katemcy Rocks.[67]

Katemcy maintained good relations with the citizens and merchants of Fredericksburg, as well as the troops at Fort Martin Scott. In the end, it was Katemcy who led his people in the exodus from Texas.

Chapter 4
Lipan Apaches

Their cruelty is so hideous as would never be accepted as historic fact. They kill their prisoners with the most frightful tortures.
—Jean-Louis Berlandier, 1828

The Apaches did not arrive in the Texas Hill Country until after the Spanish were in San Antonio. An Apache tribe, designating themselves *Náizhan* ("ours," or "our kind"), ranged through Texas, raiding and looting other tribes, as well as the Spanish and Euro-American settlements of Texas and Mexico. These "Eastern Apaches" were called the Lipan Apaches.[68] Lipan (adapted from *Ipa-n'de*) is apparently a personal name, as *n'de* means "people."[69]

As soon as the Apaches learned of the establishment of Béxar, they began to badger it. By 1720, the Spanish government was maintaining more soldiers in Béxar than had been employed throughout the conquest and subjugation of the Aztec and Inca empires.[70] The Spanish named the Hill Country "Lomeria Grande." The Spanish described the region as "a very broken country." All the country west of the Balcones Escarpment was regarded as Apachería and hostile. The words "Lomeria" and "Apachería" became synonymous.[71]

Once the Lipans moved into this area, they established a territorial claim over these lands. "The Apache concept of dominion meant that all resources within their domain became objects to be 'harvested' when needed—including buffalo, deer and even cactus pads or 'tunas.' When the Spanish arrived in the San Antonio region, all horses, cattle, food, material items or Spanish women or children were, by their very presence, resources available for Lipan 'harvest' during a raid."[72]

Fort Martin Scott was continuously engaged in combat with the Lipan Apaches, who had been living for more than 125 years in historic encampments along the upper reaches of the Guadalupe River, the Frio River, the Nueces River, the Llano River and even the Pedernales River.

For the soldiers at Fort Martin Scott, the greatest Lipan Apache threat came from the ancient Lipan encampment on the headwaters of the Guadalupe River, under the leadership of Captain Chico (Chiquito).[73]

In 1851, Colonel Thomas Staniford, commanding at Fort Martin Scott, reported that the Lipans had delivered to him "two scalps taken from the Wacoes near the headwaters of the Guadalupe River."[74]

In October 1851, Emil Wahrmund's horses were stolen from his farm on Bear Creek near Fredericksburg. These same Lipans also killed a settler on Goat Creek on this occasion.[75]

Since the Lipans often came to Fredericksburg to trade, conflict often arose among the "young rogues" of the Comanches, Lipans and other tribes gathered there. The peacekeeping role of the U.S. Army at Fort Martin Scott was often called on to deal with these skirmishes. An example is the meeting between the Lipans and the army at Fort Martin Scott on July 24, 1852. That day, the Lipan chiefs Chipota, Chiquito and Cartre explained the depredations by saying that "a few of their young men were not inclined to accept the pacific policy of their elders, especially after having secured a supply of liquor."[76]

A Plains Apache warrior.
Lieutenant J.W. Albert, artist, 1845.

Cuelgas de Castro

Cuelgas de Castro was an early to mid-nineteenth-century Lipan chief who inhabited the San Antonio and south Texas region. In 1838, he signed a treaty of friendship and mutual aid between his people and the Republic of Texas. Castro fought with the ranger companies commanded by John Coffee Hays. Castro died in 1842, and his son, Juan, became chief. Juan Castro served as a leading representative for the Indians on the Brazos Indian Reservation in the 1850s. Rather than accept removal to Indian Territory in 1859, the Lipans fled to Mexico and joined the Kickapoos.[77]

Flacco

Chief Flacco led a Lower Lipan band, who ranged from east of San Antonio to areas southwest of San Antonio (particularly Medina and Uvalde Counties). Chief Flacco and his warriors played a vital role in the defense of the new republic. From 1838 to 1840, they joined Texas militia units led by Colonel John H. Moore in campaigns against the Comanches.[78] Chief Flacco's closest association with the Texans was his relationship with John "Jack" Coffee Hays. Hays described the chief as "tall and erect, with well-shaped limbs. He gave an impression of bounding elasticity. His circlet of eagle feathers was set back on his forehead so that it revealed his black eyes and gave to his bearing a fierce alertness coupled with strength and agility. Flacco's general appearance was suggestive of the hawk and the panther." The Texas Ranger also credited Flacco with saving his life on several occasions in battles against the Comanches.[79]

Lipan Apache Warriors

Several eyewitness accounts of the Lipan Apaches are available. Of locality relevance is Frank M. Buckelew's tale of capture in 1866 and subsequent life among the Lipans.[80] Another is Herman Lehmann's *Nine Years Among the Indians 1870–1879*.[81] Clinton L. Smith and Jeff D. Smith also wrote an account of their life as captives of the Comanches and Apaches.[82] Also of note is Berlandier's *The Indians of Texas in 1830*, which contains his detailed notes of travels through the Kerr County area and the character of the Lipan Apaches.[83] This report is augmented by his traveling companion, José Francisco Ruiz, who wrote a report on the Indian tribes of Texas in 1828.[84]

In September 1731, the Lipan Apaches declared war against the Spaniards at Béxar and revealed the difference between Lipan raiding and Lipan warfare. More than five hundred warriors—each well armed with bows, arrows and metal-tipped lances—stole some fifty horses and then ambushed the pursuing Spanish soldiers. A hard-fought battle between the soldiers and the Indians took place just outside San Antonio. The Apache battle tactic was to draw out the Spanish by stealing horses, leading the troops on a chase into an ambush. Once caught in the ambush, the Spanish soldiers faced a much larger force of Apaches, all on horseback and well armed. The Apache warriors would dismount, forming a battle line in the shape of a crescent, eventually enclosing the soldiers. Although excellent horsemen, the Lipan Apaches fought on foot. Warriors would ride to the site of the battle and then dismount to engage their enemy.[85]

The Lipan Apache warrior averaged between five foot, eight inches and five foot, ten inches in height. He usually wore a buckskin shirt, leggings and knee-high moccasins. In cool weather, he wore a buckskin jacket or buffalo skin. His shirt was beaded and decorated with fringe. Typically, the Lipan warrior was mounted on horseback, using a wooden Spanish-style saddle with iron stirrups.

Apache Warrior. Frederich Richard Petri, artist, watercolor, circa 1850s.

The Lipans' warhorses wore armor—a buffalo hide was wrapped around the horses' chests to protect the animals from arrows. The main weapon of choice by the Lipans was the bow and arrow. Bows were made of "cedar wood or winter savory sticks." Later, the Lipans used mulberry wood for their bows. Arrows were generally constructed of any "hard, firm wood, which was well-seasoned and always kept in a dry place."[86] Buckelew reported that the Lipans "sometimes poisoned the arrows they used in battle, which if they did not kill a person instantly, the poison would kill the victim in a few days."[87]

The Lipan warriors were renowned for their lances. Buckelew provided a description, writing, "The lance was a long dangerous looking weapon, made of fine steel, and the blade being fastened to a wooden handle with a nice brass ferrule."[88] Berlandier noted that the lance was "usually tipped with the straight blade of a Spanish saber, 2½ feet or so in length, with a shaft 8 or 9 feet long."[89]

The Lipan warrior used a shield effectively in battle. The only description of a Lipan shield comes from Frank M. Buckelew, who lived among the Lipans as a captive.[90] Lipan shields were made from thick, untanned bull hide that was cut in an oval, soaked in water and shaped by placing it in a shallow hole to dry. When the hide had dried, it was ready to be made into a shield. Two slits were cut in each side. A loop of buckskin was placed in the slits and drawn together. Small holes were punched in the edge and a drawstring run through these, which were drawn up and evenly tied.[91]

Berlandier acknowledged that the Lipans were "skilled at warfare" but also noted, "Their cruelty is so hideous as would never be accepted as historic fact. They kill their prisoners with the most frightful tortures."[92]

In 1848, Indian agent Robert S. Neighbors unsuccessfully attempted to move the Lipan Apaches onto their long-established encampment on the headwaters of the Guadalupe River. This location has been a traditional area of occupation for the Lipans since the early 1700s.[93]

After the 1852 conference at Fort Martin Scott, the Lipans agreed to move close to Fort Mason, Texas, where the army was better prepared to enforce the peace. Their numbers were estimated to be between 300 and 500 people. In July 1852, the Lipan Apache Band of Texas resided at Fort Belknap, Texas, on the Clear Fork of the Brazos River, with an estimated number of 150 tribal members. In 1858, the Lipan Apache Band of Texas resided at Fort Clark, Texas, and River Frio area, with an estimated number of 75 to 100 tribal members. In 1870, the Lipan Apache Band of Texas resided at Fort Griffin, Texas, with 26 tribal members.

Camp of the Lipans. Theodore Gentilz, artist, 1840s.

The Lipans' identity as a distinct people began to fade. Virtually exterminated by smallpox, starvation and relentless warfare, the Lipans dwindled to a small number after 1881, and there were no serious attempts on the part of the Lipan Apaches to remain in Texas.[94]

Lipan Apache descendants presently live among the Mescalero Apaches in New Mexico and the Tonkawas and the Plains Apaches in Oklahoma. The Lipans are not a federally recognized tribe, and little of their culture remains.[95]

Today, the Lipan Apache Band of Texas membership consists of 745 members and is composed of the Cúelcahén Ndé ("People of the Tall Grass"), Tú é diné Ndé ("Tough People of the Desert"), Tú sìs Ndé ("Big Water People"), Tas steé be glui Ndé ("Rock Tied to Head People"), Buií gl un Ndé ("Many Necklaces People") and Zuá Zuá Ndé ("People of the Lava Beds"). They continuously lived in Texas before first contact with the Spanish.[96]

Chapter 5
Texas Rangers

Brethren, leave us go amongst 'em!
–Texas Ranger Reverend Clayton in The Searchers *(1956 film)*

Long before the U.S. Army established Fort Martin Scott in 1847, the Texas Rangers were assigned the mission of combating hostile Indians in Texas. Texas Rangers were in action in and around Fredericksburg in the 1830s and 1840s. It appears that Camp Houston, the site of the future Fort Martin Scott, may have been a Texas Ranger camp established in 1845. Ranger captain John Coffee Hays owned land at Fredericksburg in 1846.[97] There is a long and complex relationship between the Texas Rangers and the U.S. Army at Fort Martin Scott.

There have been ranging companies in the region now known as Texas almost as long as non-Indians have called Texas home. The modern Texas Rangers date their origins from ranging companies organized by Stephen F. Austin and Moses Morrison in 1823. These paramilitary volunteers were called by many names in the nineteenth century: rangers and ranging companies, minutemen, mounted volunteers, mounted gunmen, mounted riflemen, spies, frontier men, Texas State Troops, Frontier Regiment, Frontier Organization, Frontier Forces, Special State Troops, Special Force, Frontier Battalion, State Rangers and Texas Rangers. Their duties were essentially the same—protect the frontier from depredations by hostile forces—regardless of origin. By 1900, the ranging companies had been reorganized into a crime fighting, crime prevention and crime investigation organization, and their name had been standardized as Texas Rangers.[98]

In 1823, only two years after Euro-American colonization formally began in Texas, impresario Stephen F. Austin hired ten experienced frontiersmen as "rangers" for a punitive expedition against a band of Indians. However, not until 1835 did Texas lawmakers institute a specific force known as the Texas Rangers.[99]

On December 10, 1838, Mirabeau B. Lamar was formally inaugurated president of the Republic of Texas. Toward the Indian tribes, President Lamar's policy was just the reverse to that of his predecessor. While President Houston endeavored to maintain friendly relations with them by kind treatment and conciliatory means, Lamar thought that they should be excluded from the territory, and to accomplish this policy, he proposed to "mark the boundaries of the Republic with the sword."[100]

The Indians were not the only peril. Bandits and rustlers were scourges of the undeveloped country. The entire frontier was constantly in serious menace from the frequent forays of the several different groups of "filibusters and freebooters"[101] that loitered along the borders, seeking to carve new countries out of the big empty land. As civilization inexorably advanced westward, the demand of settlers and travelers for protection was now becoming strident and vociferous.

JOHN H. MOORE

The young Republic of Texas was incapable of funding a standing army. The available finances had been entirely exhausted, and the republic could not obtain credit. Yet Lamar was determined in his policy and at once commissioned Colonel John H. Moore to raise three companies of rangers to patrol the most defenseless portion of the frontier.[102]

The Texas Ranger organization had a complement of fifty-six men in three companies, each officered by a captain and two lieutenants, whose immediate superior and leader had the rank of major and was subject to the commander in chief of the regular army. The major was responsible for enlisting recruits, enforcing rules and applying discipline. Officers received the same pay as United States dragoons and privates ($1.25 per day); however, they supplied their own mounts, equipment, arms and rations. At all times,

Texas Ranger of 1840. *Library of Congress.*

they had to be ready to ride, equipped "with a good and sufficient horse... [and] with one hundred rounds of powder and ball."

A new breed of horse was developed to compete with the Comanches. The new stock was developed from Spanish mustangs mixed with Kentucky and Arabian strains—new mounts that would be larger, heavier and more long-winded than the Indian ponies.[103] Historian Nelson Lee noted:

> *The qualifications necessary in a genuine Ranger were not, in many respects, such as are required in the ordinary soldier. Discipline, in the common acceptation of the term, was not regarded as absolutely essential. A fleet horse, an eye that could detect the trail, a power of endurance that defied fatigue, and the faculty of "looking through the double sights of his rifle with a steady arm,"—these distinguished the Ranger, rather than any special knowledge of tactics. He was subjected to no "regulation uniform," though his usual habiliments were buckskin moccasins and overhauls, a roundabout and red shirt, a cap manufactured by his own hands from the*

> *skin of the coon or wildcat, two or three revolvers and a bowie knife in his belt, and a short rifle on his arm. In this guise, and well mounted, should he measure eighty miles between the rising and setting sun, and then, gathering his blanket around him, lie down to rest upon the prairie grass with his saddle for a pillow, it would not, at all, occur to him he had performed an extraordinary day's labor…The compensation received from government at that time was one dollar a day.*[104]

S.C. Gwynne, in his book *Empire of the Summer Moon*, described the Rangers as a "tough bunch. They drank hard and liked killing and firefighting and knife-fighting and executing people they deemed criminals or enemies. As time went by, and so many of them were killed, creating a sort of natural selection in their ranks, they got even rougher, more brutal and more aggressive."[105]

John Coffee Hays

In 1840, John Coffee Hays was appointed a captain of the Rangers. He proved himself to be a fearless fighter and a good leader of men. His Ranger companies—often mixed groups of Anglos, Hispanics and Indians—engaged in battles and skirmishes with the Comanches and other hostile Indian tribes, as well as Mexican troops, throughout the early years of the 1840s. Hays and his Rangers were involved in important actions at Enchanted Rock, Plum Creek, Cañon de Ugalde, Bandera Pass, Painted Rock, Salado and Walker's Creek. Hays gained further respect as a fighter during the Mexican-American War. The First Regiment, Texas Mounted Riflemen, under the command of Colonel Jack Hays, served with the army of General Zachary Taylor. Hays's men scouted for the army and took part in the Battle of Monterrey, Nuevo Leon, Mexico, in 1846.[106]

In the fall of 1841, when Captain John Coffee Hays and about twenty members of his company were scouting in the vicinity of the Enchanted Rock (30° 30' 24" N, 98° 49' 08" W), Hays became separated from his companions. At an unexpected moment, he was charged by Indians and, as a consequence, retreated to the Enchanted Rock.[107] Hays was pursued by the Indians until he reached the summit of this great wonder of the Southwest. Here he entrenched himself in a crevice and intended to sell his life as dearly as possible. He did not fire until it became absolutely necessary, and when he did, an Indian hit the granite. Again and again it became necessary for him to fire, and nearly every time, other Indians were desperately wounded or killed.

For a time, the Indians, who were losing heavily, fell back, and this gave Captain Hays an opportunity to reload his firearms. And in this manner, for some time, he made a desperate fight for his life. His comrades were having a fight of their own near the bottom of the Enchanted Rock, but they could hear the firing of their captain and screaming of Indians near the crest of this wonderful structure. As rapidly as possible, they fought their way in his direction; so deadly was their fire that the Indians were soon forced to flee. Those warriors who had surrounded the captain now saw the advance of the rangers and immediately retreated to the opposite side of the Enchanted Rock.

Captain Jack Hays and his men were soon again together, and another victory was added to the lists of this noble Indian fighter and his men. After the smoke of the battle had cleared away, five or six Indians lay around the spot where Hays had fought, and twice the number were found below. Three or four rangers were seriously hurt, but none was fatally wounded.[108]

On June 9, 1844, Captain John Coffee Hays was in charge of a detachment of fourteen men at the Pinta Trail Crossing of the Guadalupe River (29° 57.529' N, 93° 42.925' W). The Rangers were surprised by about fifteen Comanche warriors, who showed signs of wanting to fight.[109] Captain Hays and his rangers were attacked by a Comanche war party led by Yellow Wolf that had recently been raiding into Béxar County. Noah Cheery called out, "Jerusalem, captain, yonder comes a thousand Indians!"[110]

This became renowned as the Battle of Walker's Creek. The Comanches retreated with heavy losses. This was the first combat in which the Rangers used the Colt revolver, and it revolutionized Indian warfare. According to Josiah W. Wilbarger,[111] it is the famous Battle of Walker's Creek that is depicted on the cylinder of the 1847 Walker Dragoon model Colt revolver.[112]

MISSION CONFLICT

In May 1847, Texas allowed the German settlers near Fredericksburg and New Braunfels to make their own treaty with the Texas Comanches. In exchange for land, the Germans promised a trading post and gifts. The Rangers did nothing to prevent encroachment of Comanche lands but would retaliate if the new settlements beyond the line were attacked.[113]

Following the end of the war in 1848, the Rangers were largely disbanded, but the election of Hardin Richard Runnels as governor in 1857 meant that $70,000 was allocated to fund the Rangers under John Salmon "Rip" Ford, a veteran of the Mexican-American War. The now one-hundred-strong Rangers participated in campaigns against the Comanches and other tribes whose raids against the settlers and their properties had become common.[114]

The Texas Rangers operated under a different mission statement than the U.S. Army. Fehrenbach wrote, "The army tried to police the frontier primarily by keeping the peace. The Texans rode to punish the Indians and push them back."[115]

The success of a series of campaigns in the 1860s marked a turning point in Rangers' history. The U.S. Army could provide only limited and thinly stretched protection in the enormous territory of Texas. In contrast, the Rangers' effectiveness when dealing with these threats convinced both the people of the state and the political leaders that a well-funded and organized local Ranger force was essential. Such a force could use the deep familiarity with the territory and the proximity with the theater of operations as major advantages in its favor. This option was not pursued in the light of the emerging national political problems, and the Rangers were again dissolved.[116]

Many Rangers enlisted to fight for the Confederacy following the secession of Texas from the United States in 1861 during the American Civil War. In 1870, during Reconstruction, the Rangers were briefly replaced by a Union-controlled version called the Texas State Police, disbanded only three years later in 1873. The state election of 1873 saw newly elected governor Richard Coke and the state legislature recommission the Rangers.[117]

The Rangers were active at Fort Martin Scott throughout the Civil War and in the following years. As Ranger units were formed and re-formed for the Confederacy, these forces were transferred to battlefields in other states farther east. This created an unremitting need for protection of the people and property of the Texas Hill County. Militias were formed at Fort Martin Scott.

Chapter 6
German Adelsverein

Friedrichsburg is perhaps the most unique town in Texas. Where one year there was nothing, except roving bands of Native Americans and the next year was a town of over a thousand German immigrants, the seventh largest town in Texas by the 1850 census, far from any established road, with no means to feed itself, and with no economic justification.[118]

—Friedrich Armand Strubberg

The rationale for the establishment of Fort Martin Scott appears to lay with the German colonization in the Texas Hill Country. Immigration to Texas in the 1840s was made possible by the efforts of the Mainzer Adelsverein, a society formed for the purpose of promoting German colonization in the Americas. The Mainzer Adelsverein (or just Adelsverein) was an association of aristocrats, which perfectly described this organization of princes, dukes and counts."[119]

The Adelsverein, also known as the Verein zum Schutze deutscher Einwanderer in Texas (or Society for the Protection of German Immigrants in Texas) and later as the German Emigration Company, was provisionally organized on April 20, 1842, by twenty-one German noblemen at Biebrich on the Rhine, near Mainz.

The members of the Adelsverein hoped to solve some of the economic problems of the time and turn a profit for themselves while establishing an American trade base for Germany. After various attempts to secure land, the society finally acquired the Fisher-Miller grant on the Llano River. Prince Karl

Adelsverein. *Logo of Verein zum Schutze Deutscher Einwanderer in Texas.*

of Solms-Braunfels was sent to Texas in July 1844 as commissioner general for the society, and in December, he received the first group of emigrants, with whom he founded New Braunfels in March 1845.[120]

The Adelsverein had two objectives: one, to acquire land investments that would increase in value over time, and two, to provide a safe outlet for German emigration. This society provided safe transportation from ports of entry to colonized areas in Texas and also supported the new families until they could produce a crop and support themselves. Due to the efforts of this group, 7,380 Germans immigrated to Texas between 1844 and 1846.[121]

In early May 1845, John Meusebach arrived in Galveston. He and his small entourage rode horseback to New Braunfels, 165 miles away, finishing the trip with six overnight stops. Meusebach labored to serve the needs of the new immigrants with a diligence true to the motto on his family's crest, *Tenax Propositi* ("Steadfast in Purpose"). However, indebtedness, lack of cash, the arrival of too many immigrants in too short a time, the shortage of the necessary vehicles for transporting them to the interior of Texas, the outbreak of war with Mexico in the immediate disembarkation area, the unexpectedly severe winter and disease of epidemic proportions all hampered his efforts.

Nevertheless, while he took charge of the affairs at New Braunfels, he also founded the settlements of Friedrichsburg, Castell and Leiningen.[122]

The Fisher-Miller land grant consisted of 3,878,000 acres that covered five thousand square miles (thirteen thousand square kilometers) between the Llano River and Colorado River. Originally granted to Henry Francis Fisher and Burchard Miller, the grant was sold to the German colonization company of Adelsverein. Very little colonization resulted from the land grant, as most settlers preferred Friedrichsburg and New Braunfels, which lay outside the land grant boundaries.[123]

In August 1845, John O. Meusebach left New Braunfels with a surveying party to select a site for a second settlement en route to the Fisher-Miller land grant.[124] He eventually chose a tract of land sixty miles northwest of New Braunfels where two streams met four miles above the Pedernales River; the streams were later named Barons Creek, in Meusebach's honor, and Town Creek. Meusebach was impressed by the abundance of water, stone and timber, and upon his return to New Braunfels, he arranged to buy ten thousand acres on credit. In December 1845, on orders from Meusebach, Lieutenant Louis (Ludwig) Bene, along with lead surveyor Johann Jacob Groos and crew, constructed a road from New Braunfels to the site of Fredericksburg. The town was laid out by surveyor Herman Wilke.[125]

There is some question as to whether Meusebach's men had established Camp Houston while at the Fredericksburg site in 1845. Generally believed to have been first established by Captain Seth Eastman in 1848 as a precursor to Fort Martin Scott, the camp has been reported to be dated to 1845 by Dr. Ebenezer Swift in his letter of 1850.[126] This begs an intriguing question: who established Camp Houston? The likely prospect appears to be the Texas Rangers, either Colonel Hays or Colonel Moore, who were active in this region. It could be argued that had Camp Houston been established by the Adelsverein, the site would have a German name.

In April 1846, 120 persons left New Braunfels in twenty wagons and Mexican two-wheeled ox carts to lay out a new wagon road and survey the lands to the northwest. The convoy was accompanied by Lieutenant Louis (Ludwig) Bene and twenty troopers of the Adelsverein militia. Solms had Bene's twenty mounted troops outfitted in long riding boots, gray blouses, black velvet collars decorated with brass buttons, broad-brimmed cocked hats trimmed with black feathers and clanking sabers.[127]

After sixteen days' journey, they arrived at the future site of Fredericksburg. Meusebach opted for a valley situated between two creeks and surrounded by seven hills. As Irene Marschall King wrote in *John O. Meusebach: German Colonizer in Texas*:

Map of Fisher-Miller land grant. *Karte des Staates Texas aufgenommen in die Union 1846: nach der neuesten Eintheilung*, 1849. *Courtesy of University of Texas–Arlington Library.*

Approaching the location within sight of the Pedernales River Meusebach halted his white horse to survey the land. It was a beautiful valley, with grass knee high and fine trees in abundance, especially along the river. As he came to the water's edge, he found a large pool, in which fish and soft-shelled turtles abounded. A short distance downstream the water cut through high banks to a ten-foot-high waterfall, which spread into a crystal-clear basin. At one point the river was one hundred feet wide. Grapevines festooned high in the trees...The countryside was covered with abundant pasture grasses, with deep humus underneath, which would produce excellent farm products. Meusebach visualized sugar, indigo, and tobacco crops, noting that the climate was favorable for fruit growing and for horticultural experiments. The native grapes could be used as rootstock for improved varieties. Meusebach's father had previously sent cuttings to be used for grafting. In May 1846 Meusebach founded the community of "Friedrichsburg."[128]

Ferdinand von Roemer, being a professor of geology, paleontology and mineralogy in the University of Breslau, continuously scouted around the region, making observations that he dutifully recorded in his notebook. Near to Fredericksburg, he noted a number of bleached buffalo skulls and fresh tracks. He also wrote of the presence of large gray wolves in the village. Bears were plentiful, and bear oil was being sold briskly at a dollar per gallon by the Indians. Roemer records that each Indian often had sixty gallons of bear oil for sale. The oil was used for cooking and fueling lamps. Bear meat, he said, was very palatable, resembling pork.[129]

The Fisher-Miller land grant awarded by the State of Texas stipulated that the land had to be settled (at least in part) and surveyed by the fall of 1847. It became therefore necessary to enter the Indian Territory. The land grant comprised lands between the Llano and Colorado Rivers and constituted the hunting grounds of the Comanche Indians. Meusebach thought that regular expeditions into Indian-controlled lands should take place. Government officials, however, were unable to ensure military assistance, and surveyors refused to enter the region of the grant for fear of being attacked by the Indians.

John O. Meusebach

Baron Otfried Hans von Meusebach began as a Prussian bureaucrat and later became an American farmer and politician who served in the Texas Senate, District 22. John O. Meusebach was born on May 26, 1814, in Dillenburg,

John O. Meusebach. *Gillespie County Historical Society.*

Duchy of Nassau. As an adult, Meusebach stood six feet, two inches tall and had reddish-blond hair. Waco Indians near New Braunfels called him Ma-be-quo-si-to-mu ("Chief with the burning hair of the head"). Penateka Comanche chief Katemcy named him El Sol Colorado ("the Red Sun").

On October 24, 1844, Meusebach wrote a letter to Count Castell to express his interest in moving to the Republic of Texas in order to pursue his love of geology, botany and horticulture. He had become fascinated by Texas and had been reading everything about the area. At the suggestion of his brother, Karl, he read *Texas: The Rise, Progress, and Prospects of the Republic of Texas* by William Kennedy and became intrigued by a place named Enchanted Rock.

Meusebach had considered returning to Germany as early as November 1845, when he wrote to Count Castell and announced his intention to resign and return to Germany. Meusebach did not feel that the Adelsverein was organized enough to achieve its goals. He had survived a hanging mob at his doorstep in New Braunfels on December 31, 1846. The incident had been stirred up by Henry Francis Fisher in an attempt to usurp Meusebach's power. Meusebach was the target of intrigue, instigated by Count Castell, who sent his friend Philip Cappes to Texas ostensibly as special commissioner to provide additional funding but in reality to secretly observe Meusebach to find cause to oust him. In January 1847 in Fredericksburg, Meusebach was again the target of a coup d'état, this time instigated by Dr. Friedrich Schubbert. He again submitted his resignation to accompany a financial report to Castell on January 23, 1847. The effective date of his resignation was July 20, 1847. Hermann Spiess was named his successor.

Jacob Kuechler

Kuechler was a surveyor, a conscientious objector during the Civil War and a commissioner of the Texas General Land Office. Kuechler pioneered the science of dendrochronology to date natural events. Kuechler arrived in Galveston on July 4, 1847, on the ship *St. Pauli* from Hamburg. He was part of the Darmstadt "free-thinker" fraternity[130] of intellectuals from the universities of Giessen and Heidelberg and the Gewerbeschule of Darmstadt. They founded the Fisher-Miller land grant community of Bettina, Texas,[131] after John O. Meusebach negotiated the Meusebach-Comanche Treaty in 1847.

Bettina failed after the Adelsverein funding expired, as well as due to conflict of structure and authorities. The members dispersed to other communities, and Kuechler moved to Pedernales, Texas,[132] on the banks of the Pedernales River[133] (30° 12' 33" N, 98° 56' 39" W), to take up farming and ranching with the Lungkwitz and Petri families. By 1850, the settlement had forty-four residents of German descent. No trace of it remains today.

Jacob Kuechler. *Richard Petri, artist.*

In 1861, Texas seceded from the Union and joined the Confederate States of America (CSA). On the recommendation of Samuel Maverick, Jacob Kuechler was commissioned as a captain by Sam Houston to enroll state militia troops in Gillespie County. At the muster station at Fort Martin Scott, Kuechler signed up only German Unionists in his frontier company. He was soon dismissed by Governor Francis R. Lubbock.[134]

In 1862, Confederate authorities imposed martial law on central Texas. Jacob Kuechler served as a guide for sixty-one conscientious objectors attempting to flee to Mexico. In what later became known as the "Nueces Massacre," Confederate irregular James Duff and his Duff's Partisan Rangers pursued and overtook them at the Nueces River. Thirty-four were killed, with some being executed after being taken prisoner. Jacob Kuechler survived the battle. After the Civil War, he became a surveyor along the Devils River and the Pecos River for the International and Great Northern Railroad, as well as the Gulf, Western Texas and Pacific Railroads. In 1878, he was appointed principal surveyor for the Texas and Pacific Railway.[135]

EMIL VON KRIEWITZ

Emil von Kriewitz de Czepry is another unsung hero of the deal with the Penatekas.[136] The famous treaty made in 1847 with the Comanches by German colonizer John O. Meusebach carried with it a side request that is little known. The Indians demanded that a German settler live with them in their camp far to the west of the new settlement of Friedrichsburg (the name Friedrichsburg had morphed into Fredericksburg within a very short time). The reported purposes for this were to have this man "act as an Indian Agent" or "further the understanding between the two peoples," but perhaps the most realistic purpose was "as a hostage for the peaceable intentions of the Germans." This was the dangerous position in which Kriewitz would find himself.[137]

In August 1845, Kriewitz notified the office of the Adelsverein that he wished to join a group of immigrants going to Texas. Arriving in Texas on the eve of the war with Mexico, Kriewitz and a number of other young Germans formed a company of volunteers who joined the U.S. Army. The company was commanded by another recent immigrant to Texas, Augustus Buchel. During the time Kriewitz was with Company H of the First Texas Rifle Volunteer Regiment, Meusebach had been busy attempting to move German settlers on toward the Fisher-Miller grant.[138]

In May 1846, he established the colony of Fredericksburg on the Upper Pedernales River Valley. Meusebach was aware that to attempt settlement farther northwest would almost certainly result in confrontation with the

Comanches. Meusebach ordered that a company of guards be organized to accompany him into the grant. Kriewitz was selected to form this company. He chose mostly his veteran Mexican-American War troops and set out on January 1, 1847. Upon their arrival in New Braunfels, they discovered that Meusebach had already departed and that they were ordered to follow him at a forced march. Kreiwitz's company encountered Meusebach on his return from the successful treaty negotiations near Fredericksburg. His company received orders to guard the surveyor Richard Austin Howard, who would be surveying the grant just north of the Llano River. Following the completion of Howard's work, the company returned to Fredericksburg.

The meeting in May 1847 at Fredericksburg went well. The Comanches took part in a celebration commemorating the laying of the cornerstone for the "Vereins Kirche,"[139] and a lively exchange of trade was conducted. When the time came for the "agent," to be named, however, most individuals who had placed themselves in nomination quickly withdrew upon seeing the Indians. With few other opportunities available, Kriewitz again let his adventurous spirit take over and volunteered for the assignment.

He delivered himself to the Comanche camp of Chief Santa Anna with a large quantity of coffee and sugar as further payment on the treaty. The greeting he received was far from hospitable. Some of the Comanches had visited a trading post on the Brazos River run by a one-eyed man named Barnett. When Barnett learned of the Meusebach treaty, he realized that his lucrative trade with the Comanches would move to Fredericksburg. He attempted as best he could to arouse the Comanches' suspicions of the Germans. He told the Indians that the Germans were out to steal all of their land and their horses too. This would have undoubtedly inflamed the Comanches.

Kriewitz was taken before Santa Anna, whereupon he attempted to communicate through gesture and broken Spanish that he had come to live with the tribe. The distribution of the coffee and sugar did much to appease the Indians' concerns. As the summer passed, Kriewitz struggled to accommodate himself with his new hosts as best he could, and he succeeded in forming a friendship with Santa Anna.

During this time, survey parties were going about their work in the grant and were often visited by members of Santa Anna's band. These Comanches kept to the treaty and did not molest the parties in any way.[140]

DR. FRIEDRICH A. SCHUBERT (STRUBBERG)

Dr. Friedrich A. Schubert was the colonial director of the German colony of Fredericksburg, which was established in 1846 by John O. Meusebach for the German Immigration Company known as the Verein.

Friedrich Armand Strubberg has found a place in history between pulp fiction and reality. Just like Kit Carson or David Crockett, his sensational, somewhat autobiographical adventure stories were published early enough in his own lifetime that the man and the myth became one and the same. After killing two men in duels over women,[141] Strubberg found himself on the run. He changed his name to Schubert and decided to take his chances in the western wilderness. He claimed to have studied in Louisville, Kentucky, after meeting a German professor there and to have received the diploma of Doctor of Medicine.

In 1846, John O. Meusebach designated Dr. Schubert the director of the colony at Fredericksburg, recommended by Henry Francis Fisher. He designed the Vereins Kirche in Fredericksburg.

Before Meusebach could venture into the wilderness, Strubberg led an unauthorized armed expedition of colonists into Comanche territory. Shawnee scouts reported seeing between forty thousand and sixty thousand Kickapoos as the Llano River's group retreated to Fredericksburg. Meusebach was not deterred, and Strubberg decided to make his own journey into Comanche territory.

Schubbert and Henry Francis Fisher worked in tandem to entice immigrants away from the Verein settlements to the St. Gabriel colony that he had established in Milam County. In Fredericksburg, Schubbert instigated a failed coup d'état against Meusebach. On July 12, 1847, ninety-five colonists signed a petition urging Meusebach to remain as commissioner general. Meusebach sent a letter of dismissal from his position as director of Fredericksburg appointing Jean Jacques von Coll as his successor.

In Texas, he is still known as Dr. Schubert. American historians have had few kind words for him, and the famous John O. Meusebach even called him "a humbug and an adventurer."[142]

CHAPTER 7
MEUSEBACH'S EXPEDITION

Of the foolhardiness of the Dutchmen much has been said: because they went into the Comanches' own territory. Which they would not have done if they had known of the danger.

–Houston Telegraph, *circa 1850*

Anyone who has never been into Comancheria of the Texas Hill Country and approaches from the east is likely to think that he has reached the "Big Empty."[143] Initially, the explorer follows up along Barons Creek through gentle green valleys of excellent soil, springs and lush meadows. Within a score of miles, approaching the headwaters, the explorer is soon among the hills, canyons and boulders of stratified limestone of an ancient sea, rife with cretaceous fossils. At the pass, the pink granite of the surreal mineral region is soon mounted. Rock spires, slabs, outcrops, cliffs, canyons and domes of granite and sandstone make this a difficult passage through a fairyland landscape. One might well have imagined a Comanche or Apache behind every rock. The landscape nowadays reveals its harsh heart.

In preparation for this expedition into the land north of the Llano River, Meusebach engaged an eight-man military escort provided by the Adelsverein militia. These were veterans of the Mexican-American War, well trained and combat experienced. Roemer described one trooper as "carrying two Colt pistols with revolving cylinders, each containing five shots, and a rifle manufactured on the same principle, containing eight shots."[144]

Colt Revolving Infantry Rifle, 1850. *National Firearms Museum.*

The German party left Fredericksburg on January 22, 1847, for the Fisher-Miller grant, which lay deep in the heart of Comanche territory. In fact, arrangements had been facilitated in advance of this venture. Meusebach was delayed and followed three days later. Roemer and Neighbors followed ten days later.

The group consisted of three wagons and forty men, including Lorenzo de Rozas. As a child, Rozas had been kidnapped by the Comanches. By virtue of his knowledge of the Comanche language and the territory, Rozas was appointed guide and interpreter.

The expedition got off to an inauspicious start. On the second day, one of the men was seriously injured when his rifle exploded while on a buffalo hunt, so he had to return to Fredericksburg. Also, while building a campfire, it began to burn out of control. In futility, Meusebach's men fought the prairie fire for thirty-six hours. The earth was burned for miles around, and the event most certainly alerted any Indians in the area to their presence. Meusebach joined them in camp several days after their journey into the Comancheria began.

About ten days after the Meusebach group had left, the governor of Texas, James Pinckney Henderson, sent Robert S. Neighbors to warn Meusebach of the possible consequences of entering Indian Territory. He had been given orders to the effect that if Meusebach had already departed, Neighbors was to overtake the expedition and offer to assist in the negotiations. Ferdinand von Roemer accompanied Neighbors.

Seventeen days after their departure, Meusebach and his men encountered a hunting party of Shawnees in the immediate vicinity of the Llano River (30° 39' 41" N, 99° 06' 43" W). After communicating to the Indians in broken English, they hired three Shawnees as hunters, who told Meusebach that his expedition was under constant surveillance by the Comanches, whose tracks they had detected.

After crossing the Llano River, the German expedition advanced very cautiously. Forewarned by the Shawnees, the troop had to be vigilant,

Comanche Lookout. Captain Arthur T. Lee, artist, 1858.

prepared to meet a sudden and unexpected attack by the Comanches. Great care had to be exercised in the selection and preparing of the night camps. The expedition apparently stopped at Gamel Springs in what is now Mason, Texas (30° 45' N, 99° 14' W). Moritz Tilling wrote:

> *When a suitable spot had been found, the eight tents of the company were pitched in a semi-circle and the openings closed by the wagons, while from six to eight fires were kept burning all night in the enclosure, four men being constantly on guard duty. In the flickering light of the campfires, the different costumes, physiognomies and actions of the Mexicans, Indians, Germans and Americans presented a rather picturesque appearance.*[145]

San Sabá Encounter

Finally, the expedition encountered a party of Comanches advancing in their direction and carrying a white flag.[146] Meusebach's men were met by Chief Katemcy at today's Camp San Sabá (30° 50' 45" N, 99° 15' 42" W) on

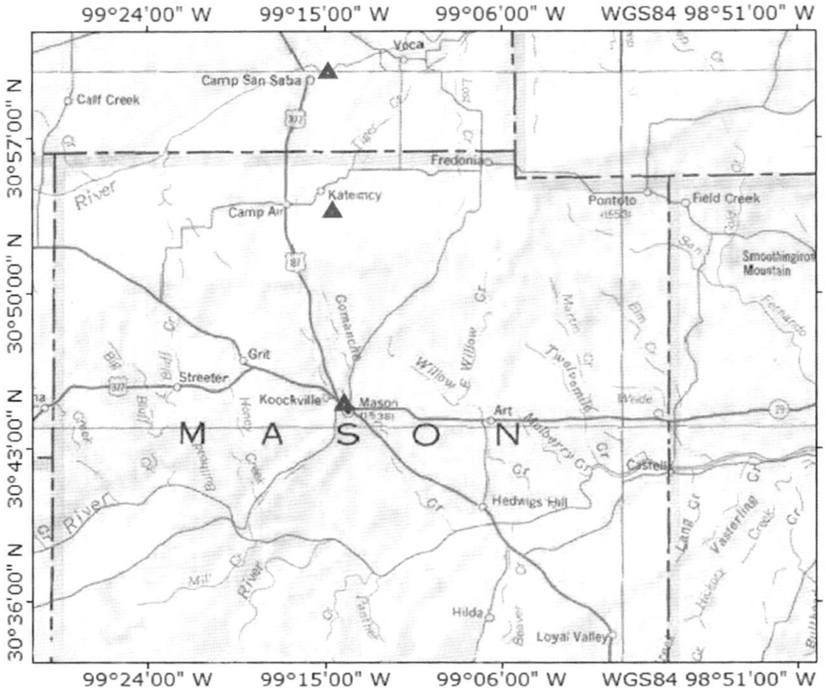

Map of Mason, Camp San Sabá and Katemcy. *Drawn by Joseph Luther, 2013.*

the river of that name.[117] This was a favorite campground of the Penateka Comanches.[148]

The following account is from an anonymous report taken from the files of two officers of the expedition who later returned to Germany. Entitled "Meusebach's Expedition into the Territory of the Comanche Indians in January, 1847," this account originally appeared in an early number of the *Magazine of Literature from Abroad*:

> *On February 7th we finally approached their wigwams on the San Saba River and here we were given a ceremonious reception. From the distance we saw a large number of Indians in their colorful array coming down the hill in formation. As we came nearer they entered the valley, all mounted, and formed a long front. In the center was the flag; on the right wing were the warriors, divided in sections and each section had a chief, the left wing was formed by the women and children, also mounted. The entire spectacle*

presented a rich and colorful picture because the garb of the Comanche on festive occasions is indeed beautiful and in good taste. The neck and ears are decorated with pearls and shells and the arms with heavy brass rings. The long hair of the men is braided into long plaits, which, when interlaced with buffalo hair, reaches from head to foot and is decorated with many silver ornaments.

As we approached the formation of the Comanche, it was requested of Mr. Meusebach that only he and few companions come nearer, and that was arranged. When our four or five men were within 100 paces, Lorenzo told us that if we fired our guns [into the air] *as an indication of our confidence, that it would make a very favorable impression. This we did and the Comanche responded in a like manner. We were greeted with elaborate handshakes and then led into their village.*

Devil Spring

The next day, Chief Katemcy led the Germans to his winter camp at Devil Spring (30° 54' 40" N, 99° 14' 55" W), which is now called Katemcy Creek.[149] On February 10, Neighbors and Roemer came upon the Meusebach expedition. Roemer wrote:

The three covered wagons which had been drawn into the center of the camp were an arresting sight in this pathless wilderness, in which up till now no wagon very likely had entered. Around these, the tents had been erected and in front of them whites and Indians mingled in a motley crowd. Even the whites were of diverse appearance and of mixed origin. In addition to a number of unaffected Germans with genuine peasant features, one noticed in the immediate vicinity a group of Mexican muleteers with the unmistakable southern facial expression; then there were a number of American surveyors, equally peculiar representatives of a third nationality, which von Meusebach carried with him in order to point out to them the land to be surveyed.[150]

On February 10, the expedition advanced deeper into Comancheria. They were met by Santa Anna on the twelfth. This preeminent Comanche chief demanded to know the intentions of Meusebach's armed expedition. After a parley and presentation of gifts to the chief, Meusebach, with fourteen companions, set out on February 14 to search for the lost silver mines at the old Spanish fort.

LOS ALMAGRES MINE

Meusebach and Roemer received permission to lead an expedition to visit the old Presidio San Luis de las Amarillas (30° 55' 20" N, 99° 45' 10" W), established in April 1757.[151] This was, after all, a high priority of the expedition because of the presidio's association with the Los Almagres Mine.[152] It was a region said to be rich in silver deposits.

On February 18, Meusebach and Roemer, with a small group, visited the area on the San Sabá River "to determine viability for a settlement" and to search for the lost silver mines.[153]

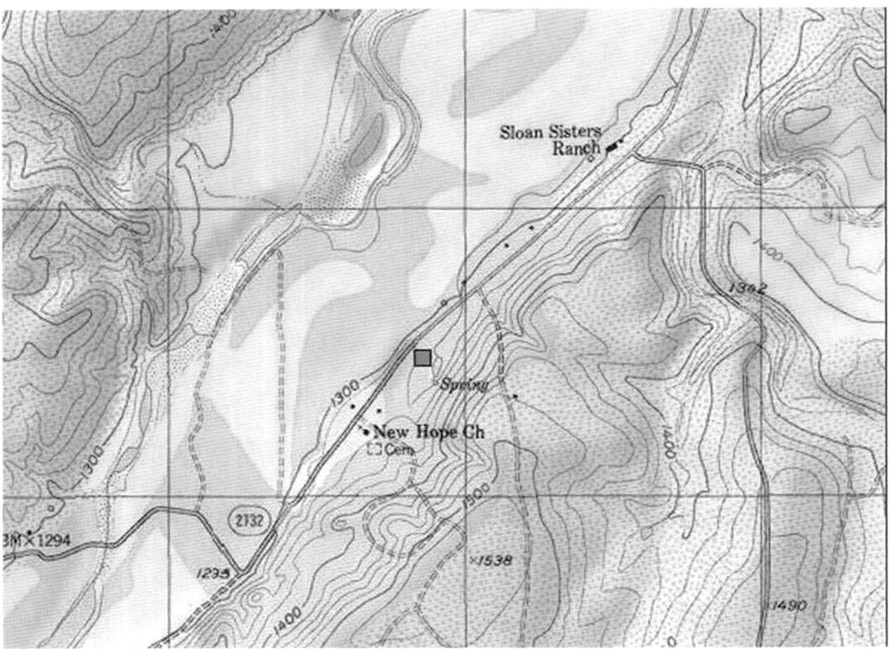

Map of Sloan Springs. *Drawn by Joseph Luther, 2013.*

In his accounts, Roemer mentioned several times a "persistent rumor among the Texas settlers that the Spaniards had worked some silver mines in the vicinity of the fort." Upon arriving there, Roemer noted the names of previous visitors who had inscribed their names on the main portals: "Padillo 1810, Cos 1829, Bowie 1829, Moore 1840."[154]

After examining the area, Roemer concluded, "One may make the claim without hesitation, that at least in the vicinity of the fort no deposits of precious metals are present." Although Meusebach had hoped that the existence of silver mines would alleviate the financial straits of the society, he wrote before his departure, "I do not really count the silver mines until we have them."

Sloan Springs

On February 27, Meusebach returned and was met by Indian scouts, who led him and his party to the "Great Council of Peace." Negotiations commenced on March 1–2, 1847, at Sloan Springs, a tributary of the San Sabá River. The location of this historic Penateka Comanche camp is on FM 2732 (Sloan Road), off U.S. 190 southwest of San Sabá (31° 09' N, 98° 55' W).[155]

Chapter 8
Meusebach-Comanche Treaty of 1847

The Germans likewise promise to aid the Comanches against their enemies, should they be in danger.
—John O. Meusebach at 1847 treaty

At the Great Council of Peace, about twenty chiefs participated, of which Old Owl, Santa Anna and Buffalo Hump were the most prominent. At the time of the midday sun, they all arrived at the prearranged meeting place, sitting down in solemn silence on buffalo skins spread out in a wide circle around the campfire.[156]

Ferdinand Roemer, in his account of the meeting, offered this description of the chiefs:

> *The three chiefs, who were at the head of all the bands of the Comanches roaming the frontiers of the settlements in Texas looked very dignified and grave. They differed much in appearance.* [Old Owl] *the political chief, was a small old man who in his dirty cotton jacket looked undistinguished and only his diplomatic crafty face marked him. The war chief, Santa Anna, presented an altogether different appearance. He was a powerfully built man with a benevolent and lively countenance. The third, Buffalo Hump, was the genuine, unadulterated picture of a North American Indian.*[157]

Texas Historic Marker—Treaty of 1847. *Photo by Joseph Luther, 2012.*

In the course of the treaty negotiations, Meusebach told the Penatekas, as translated by Jim Shaw, "I have come a long way to see you and to smoke the pipe of peace with you. I hope you will listen to the words of truth and sincerity, as it is the German's custom."[158]

Most treaties between the whites and Indians usually amounted to articles of surrender on the part of the latter. This was not the case with Meusebach's treaty. The whites and Indians were given equal recognition and dignity. The agreement was as if between two allies rather than two formerly warring factions. In exchange for $3,000 worth of presents, the Comanches agreed to allow the surveyors and settlers into the region without molestation. Also, the Indians could be allowed into German settlements and would "have no cause to fear, but shall go wherever they please." In exchange for Comanche protection from "bad Indians," it was agreed that "the Germans likewise promise to aid the Comanches against their enemies, should they be in danger of having their horses stolen or in any way to be injured."[159]

On May 9, 1847, the vested party representatives of the Penateka Comanches and German colonists met in on the Marketplatz in Fredericksburg to ratify and sign the "Treaty Between the Comanche and the German Immigration Company." The Penatekas then demanded that a representative of the German colonists serve as an in-house intermediary and live among them. Kriewitz was assigned (after volunteering) to be the intermediary and went to live at the camp of War Chief Santa Anna. In the camp, Kriewitz began to assimilate into the culture to gain the confidence and friendship of Santa Anna, who otherwise was not totally trustful of the white settlers.[160]

Treaty of Peace, depicted by the granddaughter of John O. Meusebach. *Gillespie County Historical Society.*

Lasting Friendship, sculpture by Jay Hester. *Photo by Joseph Luther, 2012.*

Treaty Between the Comanche and the German Immigration Company
May 9, 1847

Treaty

Between the Commissary General of the German Immigration Company, John O. Meusebach, for himself and his successors and constituents for the benefit and in behalf of the German people living here and settling the country between the waters of the Llano and the San Saba of the one part and the chiefs of the Comanche Nation hereunto named and subscribed for themselves and their people of the other part, the following private treaty of peace and friendship has been entered into and agreed upon:

I. The German people and Colonists for the Grant between the waters of the Llano and the San Saba shall be allowed to visit any part of said country, and be protected by the Comanche Nation and the Chiefs thereof, in Consideration of which agreement the Comanche may likewise come to the German colonies towns and settlements, and shall have no cause to fear, but shall go wherever they please—if not counselled otherwise by the especial agent of our great father—and have protection, as long as they walk in the white path.

II. In regard to the settlement on the Llano the Comanche promise not to disturb or in any way molest the German colonists, on the contrary, to assist them, also to give notice if they see Indians about the settlement who come to steal horses from or in any way molest the Germans—the Germans likewise promising to aid the Comanches against their enemies, should they be in danger of having their horses stolen or in any way to be injured. And both parties agree that if there be any difficulties or any wrong done by single bad men, to bring the name before the chiefs, to be finally settled and decided by the agent of our great father.

III. The Comanches and their great Chiefs grant to Mr. Meusebach, his successors and constituents the privilege of surveying the country as far as the Concho and even higher up, if he thinks proper to the Colorado and agree not to disturb or molest any men, who may have already gone up or yet to be sent up for that purpose. In consideration of which agreement the Commissary General Mr. Meusebach will give them presents to the amount of One Thousand Dollars, which with the necessary provisions to be given to the Comanches during their stay at Fredericksburgh will amount to about Two Thousand Dollars worth or more.

IV. And finally both parties agree mutually to use every exertion to keep up and even enforce peace and friendship between both the German and the Comanche people and all other colonists and to walk in the white path always and forever.

In witness whereof we have hitherunto set our hands, marks and seals. Done at Fredericksburgh on the water of the Rio Piedernales this ninth day of May A.D. 1847.

John O. Meusebach	*War Chiefs of the Delaware*	*War Chiefs of the Comanches*
R.L. Neighbors, Spec Agt U.S.	*Jim Shaw x mark*	*Santa Anna's x mark*
F. Shubbert	*John Connors x mark*	*Poch-an Sanachego's x mark*
Jean Jacques von Coll		*Moora-quitop x mark*
John F. Torrey		*Matasane x mark*
Felix A. von Blücher		*To-shaw-wheschke x mark*
		Nokakwek x mark

Santa Anna's group traveled to New Braunfels in August 1847 to meet with Meusebach and his successor, Hermann Spiess. Because of his assimilated appearance, the German parties did not recognize Kriewitz, whom Santa Anna had forbidden to speak during the meeting. Kriewitz communicated with the German parties by tapping once beneath the negotiating table, which prompted the German to pass a pencil and paper to Kriewitz under the table. Kriewitz was able to slip out to visit friends, but Santa Anna became distrustful of him thereafter.[161]

Years later, Meusebach passed along the comments of Texas Ranger Jack Hays as to the effectiveness of the treaty: "[Hays] was never molested nor lost any animals during his travel within the limits of our colony, but as soon as he passed the line he had losses." Hays reported:

> *On March 3, we began our return trip to Fredericksburg. Scarcely had we completed a day's journey when a company of Comanches under Santana* [Santa Anna] *with their families joined us quite unceremoniously and informed us that they wished to accompany us all the way to Fredericksburg.*
>
> *Their company proved to be of some advantage to us, since they shot several wild horses. The meat was very appetizing. On March 5 we arrived at the Llano and on the 6th we camped on Sandy Creek near the noted Enchanted Rock. This mass of granite, so named because of its formation which has the appearance of monstrous giants and wild beasts, reminded us the castles along the Rhein. The Sandy Creek has a beautiful bed of granite, its crystal clear water dashes from one shelf to another, forming many basins which are accessible by means of natural steps and offer an invitation for a bath. We found some bass in this beautiful water.*
>
> *On the following day, after a thirty five mile ride, we rejoiced when we reached Fredericksburg. It appeared to us even more cheerful because it happened to be Sunday and the settlers, arrayed in their colorful dress from the various districts of Germany, greeted us. They too, rejoiced when they*

saw us return at the head of and in peaceful association with a troop of Comanche Indians.

Not all was peaceful in the Hill County. Only the Penatekas had signed the 1846 treaty. The Nokonis, Tenawas and other Comanches did not consider themselves bound by the agreement and continued to raid in Texas. Other hostile tribes, including the Lipan Apaches, were a serious threat to settlers and travelers in this region. Fort Martin Scott was used as a base for providing armed patrols throughout the Pedernales, Guadalupe, Llano and San Sabá River Basins. This was the time of the most aggressive patrolling by the troops at Fort Martin Scott.

Chapter 9
Now the United States

Protect the lives and property of citizens, prevent "as far as practicable" Indians from the United States crossing to raid into Mexico, and finally to protect non-hostile Indians against violence and injustice.
–By Order of Major General William Jenkins Worth, 1849

In 1845, the United States of America annexed the Republic of Texas and admitted it to the Union as the twenty-eighth state. The word "annexation" played a big role in the future of Fort Martin Scott and the Indian tribes. These people were expected to pledge their allegiance to the United States with the understanding that the federal government would secure their territory and at least provide them with the moderate amount of protection the Texans had provided during the final years of the republic. Unfortunately, the United States was unable to fulfill its acknowledged responsibilities to the Texas Indians, and the tribes suffered inordinately during the decade following annexation.[162]

That year, 1845, Texas disbanded its army. The problem of frontier defense was relegated to the federal government. As T.R. Fehrenbach wrote, "For long periods, between 1845 and 1875, the federal government tried to make peace with Indians and Mexicans, along a frontier where warfare and bloodshed was endemic, a way of life. Some two hundred Texans were killed by Indians or carried off into captivity in the year 1849 alone."[163]

When Texas joined the United States, it was clearly understood that Texas was to be for Texans: Indians were not welcome in the new state. The problems of war and peace with the Comanches now became the concerns of the federal government, as was the task of persuading the Comanches to settle on a reservation in Oklahoma.[164]

Although the federal government did attempt to address the security and welfare of the Texas tribes, the annexation aspect of Texas's entry into the United States severely hampered this. Texas had retained complete control of its public lands. The lands occupied by the Texas Indians were not the domain of the United States. In turn, the United States could not apply or enforce the federal government's Indian laws. This led to the removal of provisions from various treaties that extended the federal trade and intercourse laws over Texas Indians and protected them from trespassers. Further, Texas did not acknowledge land rights for the Indians.[165]

In a monumental blunder, the United States Army fielded the First Infantry to combat the Indians. Military posts such as Fort Martin Scott hopelessly tried to match swift raiders such as the Comanches by pursuing them after an attack with wagons of heavy infantry or, worse, infantry troops consisting of farm boys mounted on plodding draft animals.

When Robert S. Neighbors[166] was appointed as "special agent to deal with Indian affairs in Texas," he was informed by Commissioner of Indian Affairs William Merrill that "it is difficult if not impossible to determine at present how far the department has the power and jurisdiction with respect to the Indian country in Texas." In effect, the United States government was virtually powerless to deal with the Indians, illegal traders or encroaching Texans.[167]

On May 12, 1846, the leading chiefs of every Texas tribe met to parley with American agents at Torrey's Trading Post.[168] A treaty was negotiated and signed:[169]

1846 Treaty With the Comanches and Other Tribes.

Articles of a treaty made and concluded at Council Springs in the county of Robinson, Texas, near the Brazos River, this Fifth day of May, A.D. 1846, between P.M. Butler and M.G. Lewis, commissioners on the part of the United States, of the one part, and the undersigned chiefs, counsellors, and warriors of the Comanche, I-on-i, Ana-da-ca, Cadoe, Lepan, Long-wha, Keechy, Tah-wa-carro, Wi-chita, and Wacoe tribes of Indians, and their associate bands, in behalf of their said tribes, on the other part.

Article 1.
The undersigned chiefs, warriors, and counsellors, for themselves and their said tribes or nations, do hereby acknowledge themselves to be under the protection of the United States, and of no other power, state, or sovereignty whatever.[170]

Following the signing of the treaty, a number of chiefs were convinced to visit Washington, D.C. The tribes desired to obtain a definitive boundary line between themselves and the Americans. Nearly fifty Indian chiefs made the trip to Washington in July 1846. Among the delegates was Penateka chief Santa Anna.

The Indian delegation went east shortly afterward and met President James K. Polk, but with the Mexican-American War just beginning, Congress had more important concerns, and the Senate adjourned without ratifying the treaty. By the time the treaty was amended and ratified in March 1847, the Comanches were certain that they had been betrayed. War was averted only when traders and Indian agents advanced credit to send part of the promised gifts. When the amendments were read to the Comanches, the meeting almost ended, but eventually they agreed to the changes. Additional money was appropriated for more gifts, but once again, a boundary line was never established.

This visit to the East made a significant and lasting impression on Santa Anna. Perhaps he was holding President Polk's Indian Peace Medal when he urged his Penateka tribe to sign the Meusebach Peace Treaty in 1847 and the Fort Martin Scott Treaty in 1850.

Santa Anna is said to have stated that before he traveled to Washington, he thought that the Penatekas "could whip any nation in the world." After, though, he realized that it was "folly to fight them," for the Americans were "more numerous than the stars and he could not count them."[171]

This was well before the Comanches made their treaty with the Germans in 1847 and demonstrates that the Penatekas were seeking a treaty when Meusebach appeared before them. It did not take much convincing.

The failure of the federal government to even discuss the issue of a boundary line for the tribes caused great disappointment among the Comanches. Tribes began to complain that President Polk "has a forked tongue…[he] sends word that he had no money to buy presents, and we must wait until the big Captains agree to our treaty."[172]

In order to conciliate the Indians, Torrey advanced Neighbors nearly $8,000 worth of goods on credit that he distributed to the various tribes in December 1846.

Meanwhile, there was a serious question over whose responsibility it was to deal with the Texas tribes—the federal or the state government. The

President Polk's Indian Peace Medal. *Smithsonian Institution, National Museum of American History.*

problem was not settled until after the Civil War. In the interim, policy was set by both, and this was confusing, so the 1846 peace treaty brought very little peace to Texas.

At the close of the Mexican-American War in 1848, troops of the United States were withdrawn from Mexico and assembled in Texas. Under the provisions of the Treaty of Guadalupe Hidalgo, the United States was duty-bound to keep Indian raiders out of Mexico, a part of the agreement that the Comanches did not respect because they had not been consulted.[173]

The War Department reorganized the army and its military geography to protect the newly acquired western frontier. This new land was a vast territory, increasing the domain of the United States by one-third. The Department of Texas, under the command of Colonel and Brevet Major General William Jenkins Worth, was assigned 14 percent of the regular army. Twenty-two companies of the U.S. Army were assigned to prevent raids against the Mexican nation and Texan settlers.[174]

In February 1849, General Worth ordered his unit commanders to protect the lives and property of citizens; to prevent, "as far as practicable," Indians from the United States crossing to raid into Mexico; and finally, to protect nonhostile Indians against violence and injustice. The mission that General Worth set into motion was to remain the basic operational orders of army troops in Texas for the entire period of the Indian Wars.[175]

The results were what S.C. Gwynne called a "breathtaking passivity" that lasted from 1849 to 1858. Soldiers were ordered not to attack Indians unless attacked or if they possessed compelling evidence that the Indians had committed a criminal act.[176]

Chapter 10
U.S. Army in Texas

Young Min! I conghratulate yiz on bein assigned to moi thrupe, becos praviously to dis toime, I vinture to say that moi thrupe had had more villins, loyars, teeves, scoundhrils and, I moight say, dam murdhrers than enny udder thrupe in de United States Ormy.[177]

–Captain Gerald Russell

Between 1848 and 1851, infantry troops established a string of company-sized posts along the frontier line. This became known as the First Federal Line. In 1851, Colonel Persifor F. Smith took command of Texas and immediately designed a new system of forts, eventually called the Second Federal Line. This new outer line of infantry-manned forts was one hundred miles in advance of the settlement line—roughly the edge of the Llano Estacado and the Edwards Plateau. The fatal flaw in this strategy was the fact that the plan left the initiative entirely up to the Indians, who would strike at times and places of their own choosing. It was not until after the Civil War that a new strategy of "large-scale converging-column" expeditions became the solution to the success of the Indian Wars in Texas.[178]

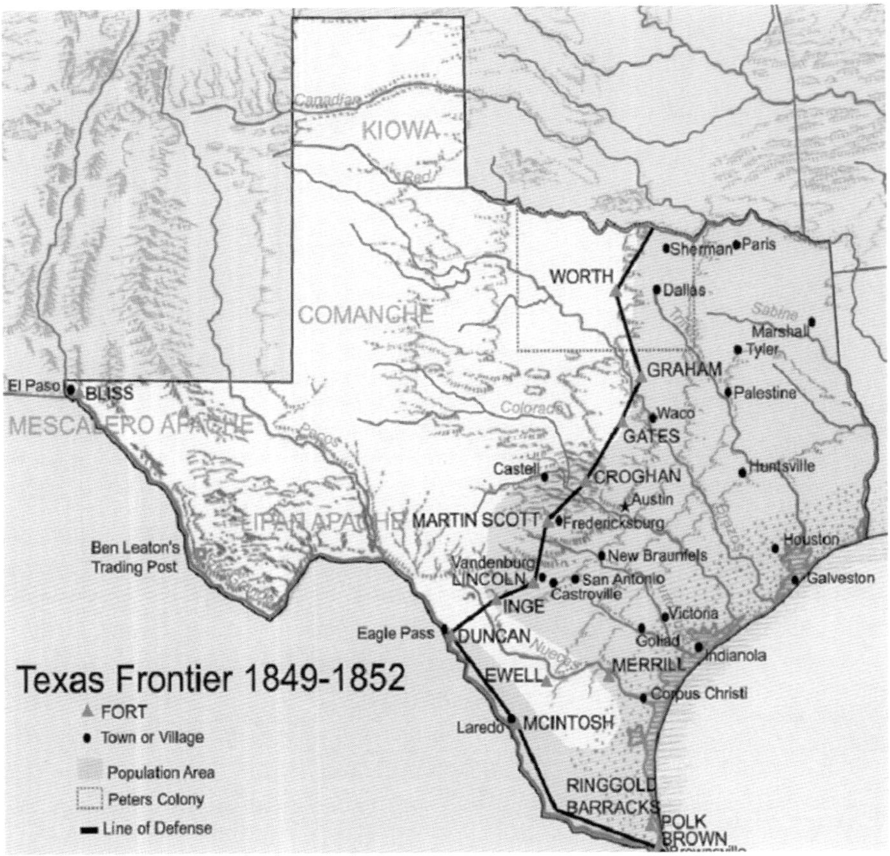

Texasbeyondhistory.net, Texas Archeological Research Laboratory, the University of Texas–Austin.

FIRST FEDERAL LINE, 1845–49

- CAMP BÉXAR, SAN ANTONIO, 1845. Established by the Second Dragoons on October 20, 1845. Served as Texas departmental headquarters because of its central strategic location and remained the preeminent military site in nineteenth-century Texas. Eventually became Fort Sam Houston. The Alamo (the Spanish mission San Antonio de Valero) was leased by the departmental quartermaster used for storage.
- FORT MARTIN SCOTT, FREDERICKSBURG, 1848. Established by the First U.S. Infantry on December 5, 1848. Originally named Camp Houston.

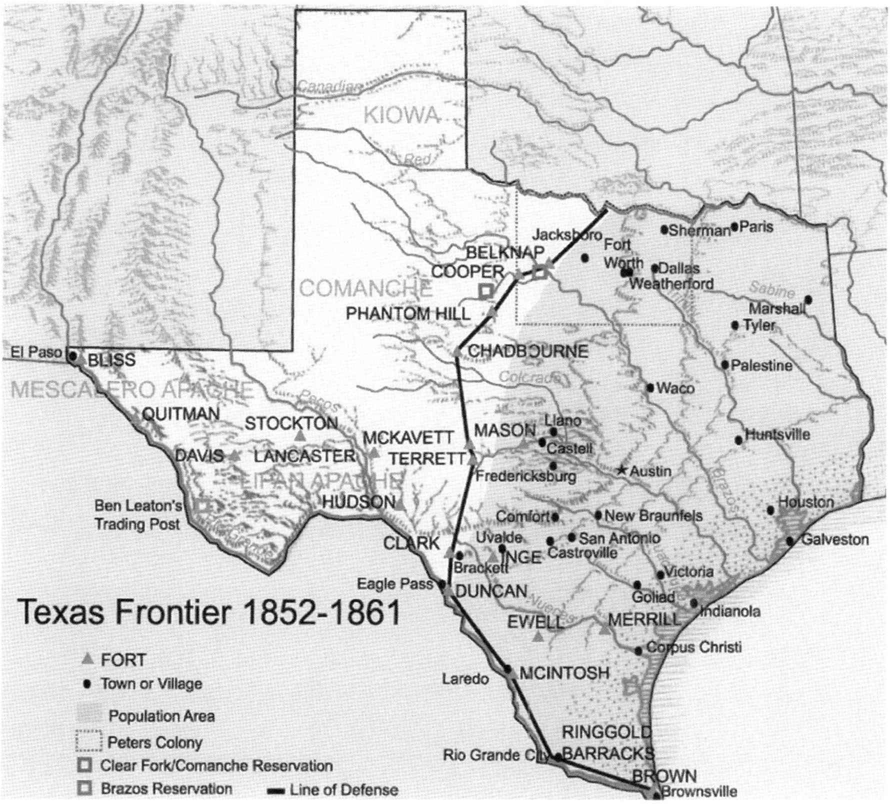

Texasbeyondhistory.net, Texas Archeological Research Laboratory, the University of Texas–Austin.

- Fort Croghan, Burnet, 1849. Established three miles south of Burnet on March 18, 1849, by the Second Dragoons.
- Fort Lincoln, D'Hannis, 1849. Established as a post (Camp Seco) on July 7, 1849, by Lieutenant James Longstreet and the Eighth Infantry. Located on Seco Creek, two miles south of D'Hannis.
- Fort Duncan, Eagle Pass, 1849. Established by the First U.S. Infantry on March 27, 1849, as a post on the Rio Grande near Paseo del Aquila, or Eagle Pass.
- Fort Inge, Uvalde, 1849. Established by the First U.S. Infantry on March 13, 1849, on the Leona River, it is one mile south of present Uvalde.

SECOND FEDERAL LINE, 1850–59

- FORT MASON, MASON, 1851. Established on July 6, 1851, by the Second Dragoons. Served as headquarters for the Second U.S. Cavalry Regiment.[179]
- FORT CLARK, BRACKETVILLE, 1852. Established on Las Moras Creek on June 20, 1852, by the First U.S. Infantry.
- FORT TERRETT, JUNCTION, 1852. Established by the First U.S. Infantry on February 5, 1852. Located twenty-five miles from present-day Junction on the North Fork of the Llano River.
- FORT MCKAVETT, MENARD COUNTY, 1852. Established as a regimental camp on March 14, 1852, by the Eighth U.S. Infantry.
- CAMP VERDE, KERR COUNTY, 1855. Established by Second Cavalry on July 8, 1855, on the northern bank of Verde Creek just outside of Bandera Pass, at the junction of the Comanche Trace and the old Spanish trail to Mission San Sabá.
- CAMP DAVANT, BANDERA PASS, 1855. Established in 1855 by one company of Mounted Rifles under command of Lieutenant J.H. Edson.
- CAMP WOOD, REAL COUNTY, 1857. Established by the First U.S. Infantry on May 20, 1857, on the headwaters of the Nueces River near the present-day town of Camp Wood. John Bell Hood of the Second Cavalry commanded here in 1860.
- CAMP IVES, KERR COUNTY, 1859. A subpost of Camp Verde, established on October 2, 1859, by the Second Cavalry. Located six miles south of Kerrville on the Lower Turtle Creek near the present-day crossing of State Highway 173.

Chapter 11
Fort Martin Scott

The Fort, as it is called, contains a few log houses for officers and soldiers quarters built by the men from timber in the neighborhood and enclosed with a stick and brush fence that don't keep the hogs out.
–Dr. Ebenezer Swift, post surgeon, 1850

Fort Martin Scott is located on the west bank of Baron's Creek, which is a tributary of the Pedernales River. Located some 2.4 miles east of Fredericksburg on U.S. 290, it is in proximity to the old Pinta Trail from San Antonio that once passed by its gates.[180] Today, the site is owned by the City of Fredericksburg. The old army post is on the National Register of Historic Places[181] and has a recorded Texas Historic Marker. The ruins are a Texas State Archaeological Landmark.[182] As such, Fort Martin Scott is afforded all the rights and protections under the Texas Antiquities Code.[183]

The site may have been originally established as a Texas Ranger outpost (Camp Houston), and the camp was on the original fairgrounds for Gillespie County.[184] The nature of this military garrison is vividly described in a letter written by Dr. Ebenezer Swift, post surgeon, in 1850.[185]

The army post was established at Camp Houston on December 5, 1848, and quartered Companies D and H, First United States Infantry, commanded by Captain Seth Eastman. Major Hamilton W. Merrill commanded the Second United States Dragoons.

The German settlers of the local area provided supplies to the army post, creating the best market for the agricultural produce of the area. The

U.S. First Infantry and Second Dragoons, 1848. *Henry Alexander Ogden, artist, published by U.S. quartermaster general, 1890.*

Germans brought corn, wheat, cured meat, vegetables and butter to sell or barter for sugar and coffee.[186]

In 1849, wagon trails bound for California arrived in Fredericksburg to obtain provisions to organize for their trek westward. Not only was the gold rush of the Forty-Niners a catalyst for this increase in traffic on the old Pinta Trail, but the opening of lands in the West also created much traffic. Many sought a military escort from Fort Martin Scott to accompany them through the hostile lands to the west. These perils included the Comanche, Apache, Kiowa, Tonkawa, Kickapoo and Wichita bands, as well as banditti and brigands.

While Fort Martin Scott never suffered a hostile attack, the troops were frequently involved in combat with Native Americans, particularly the Lipan Apaches living on the headwaters of the Guadalupe, Pedernales, Nueces, Llano and Medina Rivers.

Fort Martin Scott eventually consisted of a complex of twenty-one buildings. The soldiers patrolled the Fredericksburg–San Antonio road and surrounding area. One mission of the outpost was to protect settlers from Indian depredations. Another mission was to protect the many wagon trails headed west on the old Pinta Trail, mostly bound for the California gold mines. Fredericksburg was the last opportunity for hundreds of miles to refit and replenish supplies.

The period from 1851 to 1853 brought a number of post closures to the north-central frontier and saw a radical shift westward as the Second Federal Line formed. Fort Martin Scott ended its life as a troop post for that period but continued to serve the U.S. Army as a forage depot to provide hay and corn for government trains traveling on westward to other Texas forts. This wagon route was via the old Pinta Trail, bringing supplies up from San Antonio.[187] The Eighth Military Department renamed the camp in December 1849 for Major Martin Scott, who was killed at the Battle of Molino del Rey in the Mexican-American War in 1847.

Fort Martin Scott was inspected by W.G. Freeman on August 15, 1853.[188] The inspection report documented the number and types of structures at the fort and discussed the provisions and conditions of the quarters, subsistence and medical departments. A rough plan of Fort Martin Scott was prepared that included brief descriptions and measurements of the structures shown on the plan.[189]

Freeman reported, "This station is now kept up as a forage depot for trains supplying the upper posts." In 1853, the garrison consisted of a sergeant, a corporal and sixteen men of the Eighth Infantry under Lieutenant Theodore

Views of Texas—First Infantry on Patrol of Pinta Trail. From *A Seth Eastman Sketchbook, 1848–1849. McNay Institute.*

Fink of that regiment. It was noted that the site belonged to John Twohig of San Antonio. Freeman believed that no rent was paid for the land and that the improvements would belong to him when the troops were withdrawn.[190]

John Twohig had purchased the site in 1852 from Nathaniel Townsend, assignee of William O. Merriwether, who had been awarded 640 acres in 1845 by the Republic of Texas.[191] Apparently, the federal government never had title to the land. In 1853, Twohig leased a portion of the 640-acre parcel to C.C. Frischmeyer. The lease agreement noted that "two houses and lots, which I will point out to him at Fort Martin Scott…with fields and gardens at and about the same, as also the kitchens and stables on said lots. And that said Frischmeyer shall…and further agrees and binds himself to preserve and protect building, doors, windows, rail and picked fences, stables, etc., etc., in and about the premises known as Fort Martin Scott."[192]

Note that this lease mentions only two houses on separate lots, as well as kitchens and stables. There is no mention of additional structures at Fort Martin Scott. Six months earlier, Freeman's inspection had mapped twenty-one existing structures at the fort.

The Fort Martin Scott land remained in Twohig's ownership throughout the Civil War and years immediately following.[193] In August 1855, the *Texas State Times* carried an advertisement for the sale of the Fort Martin Scott

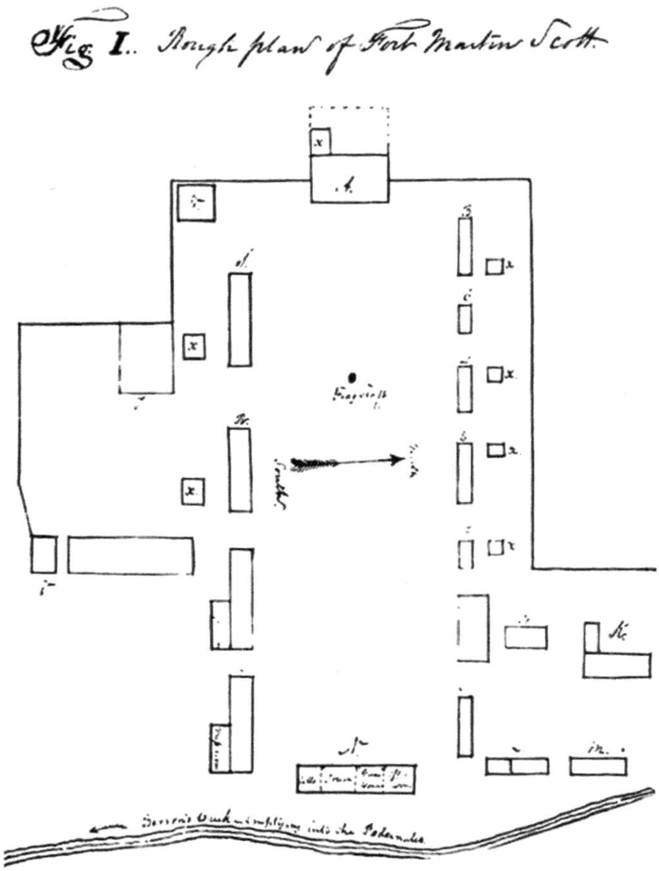

REFERENCES

A. Commanding Officer's Quarters—log building —4 rooms, 15 x 17—portico in front.

B. Officers' Quarters—adobe—2 rooms, 14 x 16—porticos front & rear.

C. Officers' Quarters—weatherboarding—2 rooms, 10 x 12—portico in front.

D. Officers' Quarters—log building—2 rooms, 12 x 14—porticos front & rear.

E. Officers' Quarters—adobe—2 rooms, 14 x 16—porticos front & rear.

F. Officers' Quarters—weatherboarding—1 room, 16 x 17—portico in front.

G. Officers' Quarters—adobe—4 rooms, 14 x 16—basement only finished.

H. & I. Sutler's Stores (private property)—built by L. G. Capers.

K. Hospital—undressed logs—25 x 12—fast decaying.

L. Laundresses Quarters and a Storeroom—log, 20 x 14.

M. Bakehouse—logs—20 x 14.

N. Guardhouse—stone—1 Offrs. room, 14 x 16—1 guard room, 14 x 16—1 light prison, 14 x 16—4 cells for prisoners, each 3 x 9—officers room now used as a magazine.

O. & P. Quarters for two Companies—each 3 rooms & a Sergeants' room—logs—48 x 16.

R. & S. Quarters for two Companies—one log & one jacal—48 x 16—One used as hay house—other, for lumber.

T. Stable—frame building—35 x 35—containing forage house & 12 stalls.

U. Storehouses—log—3 rooms, 20 x 16, and an office, 14 x 16.

V. Blacksmith Shop—adobe—14 x 16.

W. Magazine—stone—14 x 14—unfinished, requiring roof & flooring.

Note: The grounds, about ten acres, are enclosed with a picket fence except the side bordering on the creek.

[See *Southwestern Historical Quarterly*, LIII 202.]

Rough plan of Fort Martin Scott, 1853. *W.G. Freeman's Report on the Eighth Military Department.*

property. The advertisement noted that 4,255 acres of survey 197 W.B. Anderson, as well as numbers 34 and 36—the three surveys containing 5,565 acres—was for sale. The sale included a number of houses, stables and more to accommodate a regiment of soldiers.[194]

CHAPTER 12
FORT MARTIN SCOTT TREATY OF 1850

Officers of the Army within this Department are accordingly directed to carry out the spirit of this Treaty so far as can consistently be done, and it is also hoped that a spirit of accommodation may be evinced by the citizens of Texas, until such a time as the question of Indian boundary and military jurisdiction over their country can be determined upon by the proper authorities.
–By Order of Brevet Major General George M. Brooke

The Fort Martin Scott Treaty of 1850 was an unratified treaty between the United States government and the Comanche, Caddo, Quapaw, Tawakoni, Lipan Apache and Waco tribes in Texas. The treaty was signed near the headwaters of Wallace Creek in San Sabá County, Texas (31° 06' 22"N, 98° 50' 13"W), but it was named after the nearest military outpost at that time, Fort Martin Scott.[195]

Wallace Creek, also known as Spring Creek, rises twelve and a half miles northwest of Cherokee in southwestern San Sabá County. It was probably named in honor of the surveyor William "Big Foot" Wallace, who was in the vicinity in the 1850s. A peace treaty was signed by the United States government and the Texas Indian tribes on December 10, 1850, at the headwaters of the creek.[196]

The Fort Martin Scott Treaty was negotiated and signed by Indian agent John Rollins, U.S. Army captain Hamilton W. Merrill of Fort Martin Scott, Captain J.B. McGown of the Texas Mounted Volunteers (Texas Rangers) and interpreters John Connor and Jesse Chisholm, as well as twelve Comanche

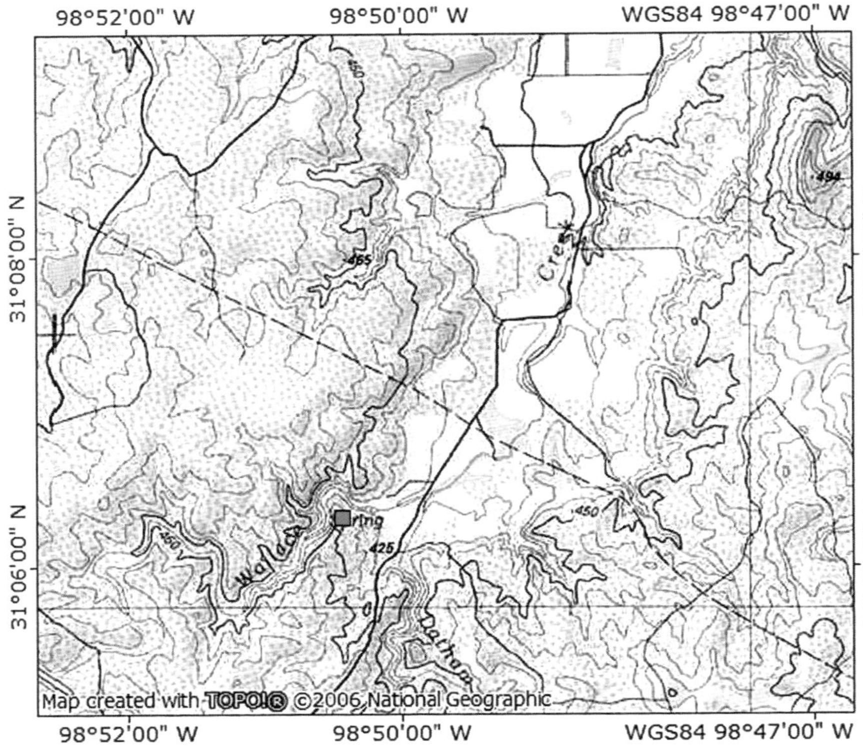

Map of Wallace Creek. *Drawn by Joseph Luther, 2013.*

chiefs, six Caddo chiefs, five Quapaw chiefs, four Tawakoni chiefs, four Lipan chiefs and four Waco chiefs. Katemcy and the peace party were said to have camped near present-day Katemcy Park, at the intersection of RR 1222 and Katemcy Road.[197]

Work on the contract was done primarily by Jesse Chisholm and John Connor, a Delaware chief, under the direction of Robert Neighbors and John S. Ford. John H. Rollins, who had fallen ill with tuberculosis, had to be carried in to the signing ceremony, and he eventually succumbed to the disease in September 1851.

On December 25, 1850, General George M. Brooke sent a copy of the treaty to Texas governor Peter Hansborough Bell, mentioning that the treaty had not been approved by the government and was essentially binding only on the part of the Indian tribes.[198]

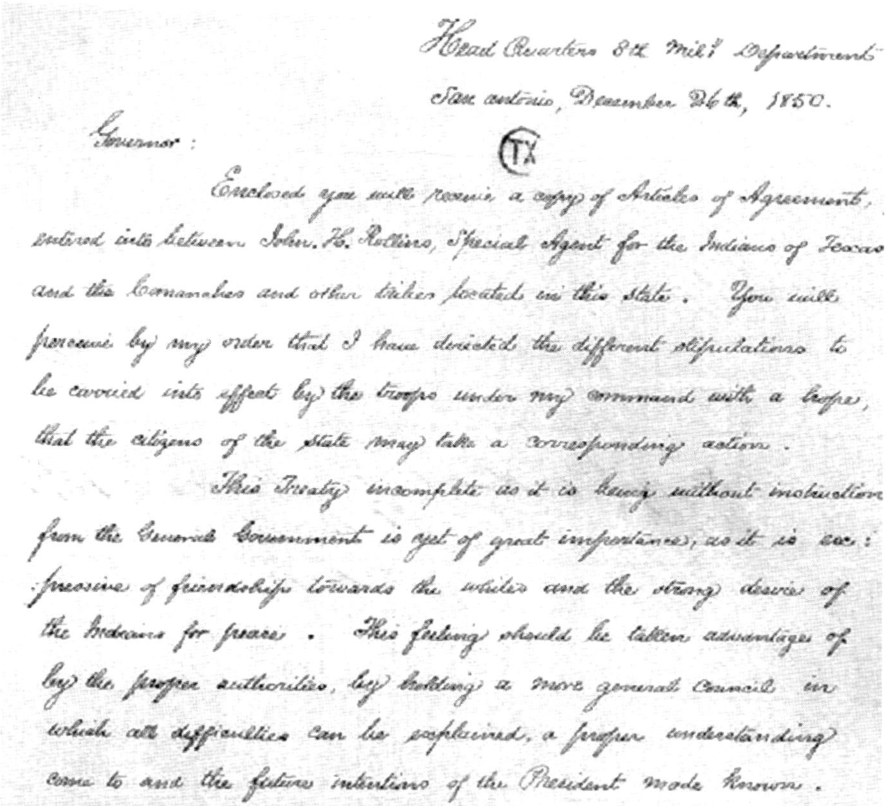

Head Quarters 8th Mil. Department
San Antonio, December 26th, 1850.

Governor:

Enclosed you will receive a copy of Articles of Agreement, entered into between John. H. Rollins, Special Agent for the Indians of Texas and the Comanches and other tribes located in this state. You will perceive by my order that I have directed the different stipulations to be carried into effect by the troops under my command with a hope, that the citizens of the state may take a corresponding action.

This Treaty incomplete as it is being without instruction from the General Government is yet of great importance, as it is expressive of friendship towards the whites and the strong desire of the Indians for peace. This feeling should be taken advantage of by the proper authorities, by holding a more general Council in which all difficulties can be explained, a proper understanding come to and the future intentions of the President made known.

In any event however, no treaty can be conformed to by the Indians, unless they receive annuities in subsistence & clothing. Missions should be introduced, farmers, schoolmasters and blacksmiths established, all of which is most desirable, evincing upon our part the great interest we take in their welfare, with the proof that we are sincere in our efforts to improve their condition.

To His Exc. P. H. Bell,
Governor of Texas,
Austin.

I have the honor to be
yr. Excellency's mo: obt. Servt
Geo. M. Brooke
Br. Major Genl. Comdg

30-1

Letter from George M. Brooke to Governor Peter Hansborough Bell, December 26, 1850. *Records of Peter Hansborough Bell, Texas Office of the Governor, Archives and Information Services Division, Texas State Library and Archives Commission.*

Treaty With the Indian Tribes of Texas 1850

10 December 1850 (unratified)
Headquarters 8th Military Department San Antonio, December 25, 1850
Orders No. 69

Article First
The Chiefs, Warriors, Captains and Councilors, for themselves and for those under their control and under their authority, do hereby acknowledge themselves to be under the jurisdiction and protection of the United States of America, and of no other Power, State or Sovereignty whatever…

Article Third
The said Indians, parties hereto, are now, and agree forever to remain at peace with the United States.

Article Fourth
The said tribes or nations, parties to this treaty, are anxious to be at peace with all nations of people with whom the United States are at peace, and it is agreed that the President shall use his exertions in such manner as he shall think proper to preserve friendly relations between the different tribes or nations, parties to this treaty, and all other nations of people…

Given unto our hands and seals—the said John H. Rollins acting for the United States, and the Indians for themselves and those acknowledging their authority—10th Day of December, Anno Domini 1850

Jno H. Rollins, Special Agent U.S. for Indians of Texas

Comanche
Po-che-na-qua-heip, Buffalo Hump
Sa-ba-hei, Small Wolf
Ca-tumsie [Katemcy, aka Ketemoczy]
T-souk, White
Car-i-wah, Never Stops
Seech-che-ni-ka, Feather

Guadaloupe
Weit-che-ki, Humming Bird
Ka-ba-ha-mo, Never Smokes
Que-ha-no
Pe-ah-tie-quosh, Rifle-breech
Mo-he-ka, Pole Cat

Caddo
Caddo John
Sa-te-wah-ah-nache
Tah-tie
The-chi-ta
Teheh-he-wok
Sam, Bead-eye

Lipan
Chi-ki-to
Chi-po-ti
Ye-keh-tas-na
Keh-rauch

Quapaw
Tish-eh-ka-wa-ta
See-ka-ta-hoa
Ho-ka
Ki-the-weh
Peh-the-heh

Tawakoni
Nes-ho-chi-lash, Traveller
Ka-ra-ki-ris, Deceiver
Heh-chi-tah, Seizer
Qui-chi-tauk

Waco
A-qua-qoush, Short Tail
Hed-e-cok-isk, Double Barrelled
Chos-toch-kah-a-wah, Hollow
Tah-to-way-chioss, Sargeant

Witnesses
Hamilton W. Merrill, Captain. Second Drag's, Bvt. Maj USA
J.B. McGown, Captain. Comdg So. Tex. Mtd. Vol.

Interpretors
John Connor
Jesse Chisholm

The 1850 Treaty of Fort Martin Scott put the signed tribes under the sole jurisdiction of the United States of America. It regulated commerce and prohibited supplying alcoholic beverages to the tribes. The tribes were required to remain at peace with one another, with the United States government and with other tribes the government deemed at peace. The tribes were to return all stolen property and captives and to cease depredations. The government made it a tribal responsibility to report any suspected activity that might violate the treaty and to assist the government in recovering runaway slaves. In return, the government would establish trading posts and give the tribes blacksmiths and schoolteachers. The treaty also required the tribes to allow Christian preachers to minister to them and to allow said preachers unrestrained travel through tribal territory.[199]

Chapter 13
First Infantry

No Mission Too Difficult, No Sacrifice Too Great, Duty First.
—motto of the First U.S. Infantry

After the annexation of Texas to the United States on December 29, 1845, the federal government became responsible for the protection of the frontier settlers from deadly raids by Indians and brigands. Fort Martin Scott was established by Companies D and H, First United States, under the command of Captain Seth Eastman.

Seth Eastman

Seth Eastman (1808–1875) was instrumental in recording Native American life. Eastman was an artist and West Point graduate who served in the U.S. Army, first as a mapmaker and illustrator. He had two tours at Fort Snelling, Minnesota Territory; during the second, extended tour, he was commanding officer of the fort. During these years, he painted many studies of Native American life. He was notable for the quality of his hundreds of illustrations for Henry Rowe Schoolcraft's six-volume study on *Indian Tribes of the United States* (1851–57), commissioned by the U.S. Congress.[200]

Left: Captain Seth Eastman. *Minnesota Historical Society.*

Below: *Dutch House in Fredericksburg.* From *A Seth Eastman Sketchbook, 1848–1849. McNay Institute.*

Seth Eastman continued to work on his illustrations of Native Americans while at the fort, and he also made numerous sketches of the "fachwerk"[201] structures in the new German settlement of Fredericksburg. Eastman retired as a brigadier general during the Civil War. In 1866 and 1867, he was commissioned by Congress to paint scenes of Indian life for the House Committee on Indian Affairs and to paint a series of American forts. He died with a paintbrush in his hand in 1875.[202]

The original First Infantry was first organized under Resolve of Congress on June 3, 1784, to serve twelve months and was continued by subsequent Resolves until it was recognized by the Act of September 29, 1789, as the "Regiment of Infantry" in the service of the United States. The Act of April 30, 1790, more fully completed its organization, and when a second regiment was formed under the Act of March 3, 1791, the older organization became the "First Regiment of Infantry."

During the Mexican-American War, a part of the First Infantry regiment continued to Jefferson Barracks, Fort Scott, Missouri, and to Fort Snelling, Minnesota. Companies C, E, G and K, under Lieutenant Colonel Henry Wilson, joined General Zachary Taylor in northern Mexico and did gallant service at the Capture of Monterey. When General Taylor sent all his regulars to join General Winfield Scott early in the year 1847, this battalion went with them and was present at the Siege of Vera Cruz (March 9–28, 1847), and it was afterward designated as the garrison of the city and castle, where it remained until the end of the war. It was then stationed on the line of the Rio Grande, where it remained for many years.[203]

Equipment

Assigned to Fort Martin Scott in 1848, members of the First Infantry probably were issued the .54-caliber Model 1841. Following the Mexican-American War, the Model 1842 musket became the service-standard small arm for the infantry and other foot troops. The Regiment of Mounted Rifles was equipped with the M1841 rifle for service on the frontier. Until the Mexican-American War, it was provided only to militia rifle companies in various states. The Model 1841 was made by Harpers Ferry Armory from 1846 to 1855. The weapon has a thirty-three-inch browned barrel, which was made without provision for attaching a bayonet. The walnut stock is

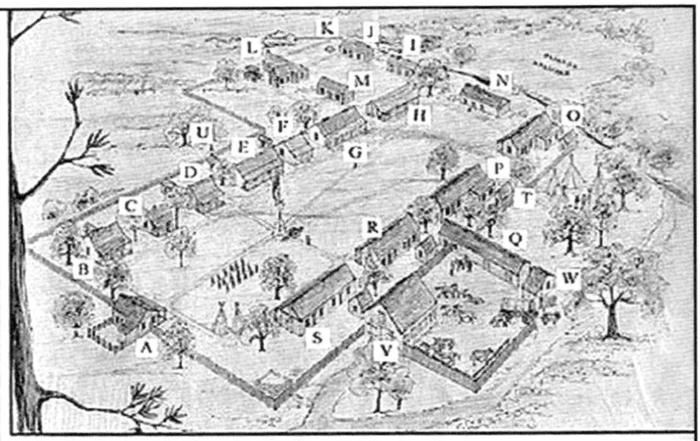

A Guide To Your Walk Around Fort Martin Scott

A. Post Commanders' Quarters/ Brautigams' Bier Garten
Commanders Quarters was a log structure approx. 34' x 30' in size, with porches front and rear. In the 1870's & 1880's, this was the general location of John Brautigam's saloon, store, and dancehall. Artifacts found at this site range from glass chards to bullet casings to ceramic pieces.

B. Officers Quarters
Adobe structure approx. 28' x 32' with porches front and rear. This structure could have housed a married officer and his family. Turnover in these quarters was frequent.

C. Officers Quarters
This structure was small only 20' x 24', framed with weatherboard exterior.

D. Officers Quarters
Another log structure measuring approx. 24' x 28'.

E. Officers Quarters
This was the last reconstructed officers quarters, being completed in the early 1990's. Originally this building had two 14' x 16' rooms with a dogtrot hallway as you see today. No major artifacts were found on this site during archeological digs in the mid 1980's.

F. Officers Quarters
Another small framed structure measuring only 16' x 17'.

www.fortmartinscott.com

G. Officers Quarters
Like Building B & E this was also an adobe structure 28' x 32' in size. The layout indicated two family use. Depending on how many officers were at the Fort at a given time and their rank, an officer and his family might have had complete use of such a building.

H. & M. Sutlers Store/Warehouse
These structures were the soldiers' source for non-government issued items, such as tobacco, etc. Both were weatherboard exteriors. Later the Brautigams built a barn at this part of the old fort.

I. Laundress Quarters
Log structure 20' x 14'. Often wives of enlisted men performed these duties.

J. Bakehouse
Log structure approx. 20' x 14', this was one of the first structures built at the fort.

K. Bake Oven
You can still see remnants of the foundation of the 12' x 12' oven.

L. Hospital
This structure was listed in the 1853 report as a 12' x 25' log structure that was "fast decaying". In a 1986 archeological survey, surface investigations found historic and prehistoric artifacts but no materials related to hospital activity.

www.fortmartinscott.com

Fort Martin Scott brochure. *Fort Martin Scott Museum Association.*

distinguished by a large patchbox on the right side of the butt. Sometimes called the "Mississippi Rifle," it owes this name to the successful use of the weapon by a Mississippi rifle regiment under the command of Jefferson Davis during the Mexican-American War.

The First Infantry was ill-suited to the task of fighting the Indians. On foot, these troops were hopeless against mounted warriors who were equipped with bows and lances. For maneuverability, the infantry was hauled to a battle by wagon, much as the truck would later be used in World War II. The rocky hills of the region made this a very difficult task. The infantry was mounted a few times, but on less than capable draft or plow horses.

Fort Martin Scott had no palisaded wall. It was a fort in name only, and the First Infantry was not intended to defend it but rather to build and staff it.

Posts

The First U.S. Infantry did not stay long at Fort Martin Scott. After performing routine scouting duties in the Hill Country around the Fort, the troops were ordered back to San Antonio and then to the Leona River (near present Uvalde) and the Rio Grande to establish outposts. Eastman's company arrived at the "Post on the Leona" (Fort Inge) in late March 1849.

Surrender

Texas seceded from the Union on February 1, 1861, and appointed commissioners to confer with General David E. Twiggs in regard to the surrender of all government property and the removal of all U.S. troops from the state. General Twiggs was relieved from the command of the Department of Texas on January 28 and was succeeded by Carlos Adolphus Waite at Camp Verde, who found everything military in a chaotic condition and devoted his whole energy to getting his troops safely out of the state and back into loyal territory.[204] Five companies of his own regiment—A, G, H, K and I—were still in Texas, with the remainder being in the Indian Territory. The Texas companies were ordered to rendezvous with other troops of the department at Green Lake, twenty miles from Indianola, and succeeded in reaching that place. Companies A, H and I got safely away, but the noncommissioned staff and band, along with Companies G and K, were captured on April 25 on transports at Saluria, Texas, by the Texan forces. They were immediately paroled, promising not to serve against the Confederates until exchanged, and sailed on the schooner *Horace*, reaching New York on May 31.[205]

Chapter 14
Second Dragoons

The Dragoons had quite a brush with about 40 Comanches. They took the Indians prisoners, but not until after an obstinate resistance had been made.
–the Picket Guard, May 21, 1847

At the end of the Mexican-American War in 1848, the U.S. Army's Second Dragoons stayed in Texas from 1848 to 1855.[206] These troops were essential to the development of the Texas frontier, and Fort Martin Scott was that frontier.

Special Forces

Trained to fight mounted or on foot, Dragoons were superb in unconventional warfare. Unlike John Wayne's cavalry that charged with pennants flying and bugles sounding, the dragoons went in very heavily armed and were skilled at stealthy infiltration—the "Special Forces" of the Hill Country. There were no Napoleonic battlefield formations here. These troopers would make slashing attacks with massive firepower, overwhelming the enemy—shock and awe. Their *ésprit de corps* resulted from their exploits on the battlefield. The Dragoons took great pride in their orange piping and hat cords, which set them apart from the cavalry.[207]

Troops of the U.S. First Infantry and Second Dragoons. Henry Alexander Ogden, artist, published by U.S. quartermaster general, 1890.

Troopers of the Second Dragoons in Texas were stationed at the following frontier posts in January 1850: Company A at Fort Croghan in Burnet, Company B at Fort Martin Scott in Fredericksburg and Company C at Fort Inge in Uvalde. Also located in Texas was Company F at Fort Worth, Company G at Fort Lincoln in D'Hannis and Company I at Fort Graham in Hillsboro.[208]

Dragoons would regularly patrol from these army posts, covering vast distances. It was not unusual for a mounted patrol to cover three hundred miles or more. The army infantry would garrison the forts. These Second Dragoons and the First Infantry had fought side by side in the Mexican-American War and now fought out of Fort Martin Scott.

Equipment

The Second Dragoons carried the distinctive shortened rifle, called a "musketoon." The U.S. Model 1847 Cavalry Musketoon was manufactured from 1848 to 1854 at the U.S. Springfield Arsenal. This was the first official percussion musketoon produced by the United States that was not a flintlock or conversion. It was a .69-caliber, percussion (cap and ball) muzzleloader. Officers would often instruct their men to load these musketoons with a double charge: two .63-caliber balls and six .31-caliber buckshot (known as buck and ball).[209]

The Second Dragoons were also equipped with the Colt Dragoon handgun, carried in a saddle holster. It was a percussion revolver, and its ammunition was in three components: the percussion cap, the ball shot and the black powder. It was a six-shot revolver and was one of the most powerful handguns of its day. The Colt Dragoon saw a lot of active service during the Mexican-American War. The huge Colt, with its tremendous stopping power, continued to be carried by the Texas Rangers fighting the Apaches and Comanches. The firepower of the Colt Dragoon .44 percussion revolver in the 1850s is on par with today's modern .357 Magnum.

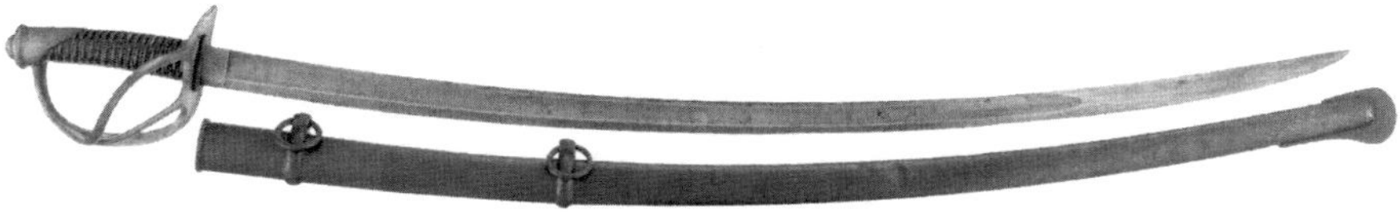

Ames Model 1840 cavalry saber. *Joseph Luther Collection.*

Dragoons also carried the Ames Model 1840 cavalry saber ("Old Wrist Breaker"). Designed for slashing, the M1840 had a ridge around its quillon, a leather grip wrapped in wire (rather than grooves cut into the wooden handle) and a flat, slotted throat. It was forty-four inches long, with a thirty-five-inch blade, and weighed roughly two and a half pounds.

HAMILTON WILCOX MERRILL

Major Hamilton Wilcox Merrill commanded the Second Dragoons at Fort Martin Scott in 1850. After participating in the Battle of Molino del Rey on September 8, 1847, he was brevetted major for gallant conduct. He also fought in the capture of Mexico City in the Mexican-American War. Merrill remained in Texas, and in the summer of 1850, he was sent to command Fort Martin Scott. At this post, he assisted in negotiating a treaty with the Indians on Spring Creek, near the San Sabá River.

Company B of the Second Dragoons, under the overall command of Captain (Brevet Major) Hamilton W. Merrill, was transferred from Fort Martin Scott to Fort Mason on July 6, 1851. They are credited with the construction of this army post. Headquarters of the Second Dragoons were at Fort Mason from December 23, 1852, to April 30, 1853, commanded by Major (Brevet Colonel) Philip St. George Cooke.[210]

ST. GEORGE COOKE

On January 12, 1853, Lieutenant Colonel St. George Cooke, commander of the Second Dragoon Regiment at Fort Mason, engaged the Lipan Apaches near the headwaters of the Guadalupe River.[211] The site of this battleground is near the Kerr Wildlife Management Area on FM 1340, some twenty miles west of Kerrville.

Cooke went on numerous trips of exploration into the "Far West" with the Dragoons. As captain in command of two hundred Dragoons, he disarmed and arrested Colonel Snively's Republic of Texas Company of about one hundred men, who were attempting to disrupt trade along the Santa Fe Trail, in what was described as the Second Texas Santa Fe Expedition. During the Mexican-American War, he led the Mormon Battalion from Santa Fe to California, receiving a brevet promotion to lieutenant colonel for his service in California. In the Second U.S. Dragoons, he defeated the Jicarilla Apaches in Ojo Caliente, New Mexico, in 1854. Cooke was in the 1855 Battle of Ash Hollow against the Sioux and was sent to keep the peace in "Bleeding Kansas" in 1856–57. Acquainted with Brigham Young, Cooke took part in the Utah Expedition of 1857–58, after which he was promoted to colonel and assigned command of the Second U.S. Dragoons. He was an observer for the U.S. Army in the Crimean War and commanded the Department of Utah from 1860 until 1861. He is noted for his authorship of an army cavalry manual and is sometimes called the "Father of the U.S. Cavalry." His service in the Civil War was significant but was eclipsed in prominence by the contributions made by his famous son-in-law, J.E.B. Stuart, to the Confederate States Army.

Fort Mason

As the frontier was pushed relentlessly westward, some army posts were bypassed and abandoned. During 1853, Forts Croghan, Graham, Worth and Martin Scott were forsaken in Texas. The mission of the Second Dragoons shifted, and protection of the westward-bound wagon trails became imperative. At the end of that year, the companies in the Hill Country were stationed as follows: Company A at Fort Mason, F at Fort McKavett and G at Fort Terrett—all along the trail west.[212]

Fort Mason, at the village of Mason, was the center of Dragoon operations in the Hill Country. Fort Mason's location on Post Oak Hill (30° 44.362' N, 99° 13.795' W), near Comanche and Centennial Creeks in the northern part of what was then Gillespie County, was chosen by Lieutenant Colonel William J. Hardee on July 6, 1851. Hardee left the actual establishment of the post to Major Hamilton W. Merrill and Companies A and B of the Second Dragoons. With the withdrawal of the Second U.S. Dragoons, Fort Mason became the headquarters for U.S. Army Second Cavalry in 1856.[213]

The Second Dragoons were withdrawn from Texas in 1855. This regiment had a record of distinction in the Texas Indian Wars. The men went on to fight in the Indian Wars on the Great Plains. Today, the Second Dragoons continue to serve the U.S. Army as the Second Stryker Cavalry Regiment in Afghanistan.

CHAPTER 15
EIGHTH INFANTRY

All battles and all wars are won in the end by the infantryman.
–Field Marshal Earl Wavell

On the eve of the war against Mexico, the Eighth Infantry was transferred to Texas. The regiment fought with General Zachary Taylor's army as he drove south from Corpus Christi to Monterrey, taking heavy losses but winning high regard for its role in eight engagements against Mexican troops. After the war, the Eighth Infantry was deployed in Texas and New Mexico against various bands of Apache Indians. Organized into ten companies, the regiment was assigned the primary responsibility for protecting the trail between San Antonio and Santa Fe. By January 1849, the Eighth had been distributed among the forts and camps of Texas, occupying them for the next twelve years. Among the posts of the Eighth Infantry was Fort Martin Scott.[211]

Fort Martin Scott was occupied by Company K in 1849 and 1850; Headquarters and Companies C, E, G and K in 1851; Headquarters and Companies G and K in 1851; and Company G in 1853. Company K, captain John Beardsley commanding, was reported at Fort Martin Scott in 1851 and was soon joined by Companies C, E and G. The Headquarters of the Eighth Infantry was reported at Fort Martin Scott on May 31, 1851. Companies C and E were soon transferred to Fort Croghan. Company B, commanded by Lieutenant Colonel Isaac Reeves, arrived at Fort Martin Scott on February 14, 1852. The Headquarters staff, with Companies B,

G and K, left Fort Martin Scott on February 15 en route to the head of the Limpia (Fort Davis). Company A left Fort Chadbourne on December 22 and reached camp on Grape Creek, near Fort Martin Scott, on the thirty-five. Company A then moved to San Antonio on January 1, 1854.[215]

The regimental commander, Major Collinson Read Gates, died of cholera at Fort Martin Scott. Fort Gates and the adjoining town of Gatesville were named for this hero of the Mexican-American War.

JAMES LONGSTREET

In 1849, Lieutenant James Longstreet came to Texas, where he was assigned to Company G of the Eighth Infantry. He spent the summer of 1849 at Fort Lincoln,[216] southeast of Fort Martin Scott. The old military road of that era ran from Fort Mason to Fort Martin Scott, Camp Verde and Fort Lincoln, passing through Center Point and Bandera Pass along the way. Longstreet was assigned to Fort Martin Scott at Fredericksburg in 1851.[217]

James Longstreet in *Harper's Weekly*, July 9, 1864.

Longstreet served with distinction in the Mexican-American War with the Eighth U.S. Infantry. He received brevet promotions to captain for Contreras and Churubusco and to major for Molino del Rey. In the Battle of Chapultepec on September 12, 1847, he was wounded in the thigh while charging up the hill with his regimental colors; falling, he handed the flag to his friend, Lieutenant George E. Pickett, who was able to reach the summit.

After the Mexican-American War and his recovery from the Chapultepec wound, Longstreet and his new wife served on frontier duty in Texas, primarily at Fort Martin Scott near Fredericksburg and Fort Bliss in El Paso. He performed routine patrols and also served as major and paymaster for the Eighth Infantry from July 1858 onward.

Though tension between the states was building, Longstreet was not an avid secessionist, though he was a proponent of the doctrine of states' rights. He resigned from the U.S. Army in June 1861 to cast his lot with the Confederacy in the Civil War. Longstreet was one of the foremost Confederate generals of the American Civil War and the principal subordinate to General Robert E. Lee, who called him his "Old War Horse."[218]

RICHARD IRVING DODGE

Second Lieutenant Richard Irving Dodge, an 1848 West Point graduate assigned to the Eighth Infantry, was stationed at the Fort Martin Scott in April 1851. That came at a time when the post and the nearby community amounted to the last vestiges of civilization for westbound travelers. Beyond Fredericksburg lay only wild, open country and hostile Indians.[219]

It is reported that Dodge was "hoodwinked" by the Lipan Apaches. Camped near Fort Martin Scott, these warriors gave every evidence of being friendly. One day, while out quail hunting with his dog near the Fort, Dodge noticed a small group of Lipans following behind him. They had never seen a shotgun and were amazed by Dodge's ability to hit such a small target on the wing. Pleased with their admiration, Dodge was eager to show them his equipment.

The Lipan chief invited Dodge to visit their village on the headwaters of the Pedernales, where the chief reported that there was an abundance of turkey and quail. Dodge return to Fort Martin Scott and requested permission from the commander, Lieutenant Colonel Thomas Staniford.

After riding out to the Lipan ranchería, Dodge set up his tent and waited. After a week, the chief appeared to warn him, in Spanish, that some of his young warriors had "bad hearts" toward the white men. Taking the hint, Dodge hastily returned to Fort Martin Scott.

Back at the post, he soon learned that during his absence, the Lipans had been raiding and murdering in the vicinity. The chief's visit to Fort Martin

Scott had been a ruse and a reconnaissance mission to learn how much military force could be put into the field. The chief's invitation to Dodge was an impromptu diversionary tactic.[220]

In January 1852, Lieutenant Dodge commanded a last winter patrol from Fort Martin Scott, which was about to be closed. In February, Dodge and his troops helped construct Fort Mason, the successor to Fort Martin Scott. The next month, Dodge was given the same construction task for Camp Johnston on the Concho River. By June, he was at Fort Chadbourne.

Dodge was a career army officer who served many years in the western Plains and participated in a number of the conflicts with the indigenous Indians. In 1882, he published *Our Wild Indians: Thirty Three Years Experience Among The Red Men of the Great West*,[221] an acclaimed primary source about U.S. Army operations of the time and the lives of the Native American warriors of the plains. Dodge's book is a testament to the contrasting cultural concepts embedded in the Indian polices of the time:

> *One of the first and most necessary steps towards the civilization of any savage people is to establish and enforce a code of laws, but to do this we must necessarily give up the pet idea of many humanitarians. We cannot make laws for other "independent nations," and must elect either to let the "independent nations" die out in ignorance and squalor, or to throw overboard the whole system, treaties and all.*[222]

THE EIGHTH AT THE OUTBREAK OF THE CIVIL WAR

At the time of the outbreak of the Civil War, the terms of surrender, which General David Emanuel Twiggs[223] negotiated as commander of the U.S. Army's Department of Texas, stated that "all United States troops stationed in New Mexico and Texas, be allowed to leave with the full honors of war, and not to be molested whatsoever on their route." In the West, seven companies of the U.S. Eighth Infantry were posted at Fort Davis, Texas, and Fort Stanton, New Mexico. The Eighth United States Infantry Band was stationed in San Antonio at that time.

Under the command of Lieutenant Colonel Isaac Reeves, the seven companies of the Eighth U.S. Infantry were captured en route to San Antonio.[224] Company C, upon entering the plaza at San Antonio on April 22, was surrounded by an overwhelming force and obliged to surrender.

Companies A and D were captured at Indianola on April 24, and Companies B, E, F, H and K, under Lieutenant Colonel Reeves, were captured near San Lucas Springs, about twenty-two miles west of San Antonio, on May 9. Company G had been broken up. The officers of Reeves's battalion were not paroled as the others had been but rather were, with one or two exceptions, held prisoners at San Antonio for about nine months, when they were exchanged. The enlisted men were held until February 25, 1863, during which time they were divided into squads and removed to Prison Canyon POW Camp at Camp Verde, Texas.[225]

Chapter 16
Second Cavalry

Around her hair she wore a yellow ribbon
She wore it in the springtime
In the merry month of May
And if you ask her why the heck she wore it
She wore it for her soldier who was far far away
—military song by George A. Norton

Jeff Davis's Own

Indian raids had become increasingly severe by the early 1850s. By 1853, the garrison at Fort Martin Scott had been abandoned as the U.S. Army posts moved westward. Fort Mason became the next post to the west and Camp Verde the next to the southeast. Fort Martin Scott, now closed, was only an ephemeral artifact serving as a forage station.

Settlers were confronted by the terrifying peril of horrific Indian attacks from Comanche, Lipan Apache and Kiowa raiding parties. In response to this frontier warfare, the Second United States Cavalry was organized specifically for service on the Texas frontier. Jefferson Davis, secretary of war for President Franklin Pierce, personally handpicked the officers of the Second Cavalry.[226]

Known as "Jeff Davis's Own," most of the officers, like Davis, were West Point graduates and southerners. The regiment was renowned for the sixteen general officers produced in the six and a half years of its existence. Eleven of these became Confederate generals, and the Second Cavalry supplied half (or four) of the full generals of the Confederate army: Albert Sidney Johnston, Robert E. Lee, Edmund Kirby Smith and John Bell Hood. Earl van Dorn became a major general in the Confederate forces. George H. Thomas stayed with the U.S. Army, becoming a major general and commander of the Army of the Cumberland.[227]

Robert E. Lee

Robert E. Lee. *From Frank Moore's* Portrait Gallery of the War *(D. Van Nostrand, 1865).*

Robert E. Lee arrived in Texas as part of the Second Cavalry Regiment as the second ranking officer after Colonel Johnston. He soon assumed command of the regiment in San Antonio in May 1857. Lieutenant Colonel Lee quickly grasped the theater of operations. Plans for extensive patrolling, rapid communications, frequent contacts and reliefs and strong reserves for possible pursuits were carefully prepared. The new strategy was to cover the entire frontier by continuous scouting of each river crossing, bank and bottom. The patrols were scheduled so that they appeared random and without pattern. More importantly, for the first time, these patrols were ordered to be aggressive. Whenever the troopers cut a trail, they were to immediately pursue and destroy the Indians in battle—search and destroy. The typical Second Cavalry patrol traversed six hundred miles and remained in the field for thirty days.[228]

EQUIPMENT

Equipment for the newly formed Second Cavalry was the subject of a Cavalry Equipment Board study. Three squadrons of the regiment were armed with the Springfield rifled carbine. One squadron of the Second Cavalry was armed with removable-stock carbine, with a barrel ten or twelve inches long. Another squadron of the Second Cavalry was armed with the breech-loading Perry carbine. Colt's .36-caliber navy revolvers and dragoon sabers were issued to all troopers.[229] Horses were purchased in Ohio, Indiana and Kentucky at an average price of $150. Companies of the Second Cavalry each had matching horses of different coloring.[230]

To add further distinction, the War Department specified that the uniform jacket yellow trim be worn instead of the orange of the Dragoons or the dark green of the Mounted Rifles. The stripes on the uniform trousers were also yellow. This uniform specification began the "yellow leg" tradition of the cavalry.[231]

TEXAS

The Second Cavalry Regiment, numbering 750 men and eight hundred horses, departed Fort Jefferson, Missouri, on October 27, 1855. The route was through Missouri, Arkansas, Oklahoma and into Texas, arriving at Fort Belknap on December 27, 1855. Enduring freezing weather consistent with the "Little Ice Age,"[232] with temperatures well below zero, the Second Cavalry had 113 oxen freeze to death the night they arrived at Fort Belknap.[233]

Upon encampment of the Second Cavalry at Fort Belknap, orders were received assigning the companies to stations. The regimental headquarters, with Companies B, C, D, G, H and I, were directed to occupy the old post of Fort Mason (30° 44' 25" N, 99° 14' 52" W).[234] Companies A, E, F and K were directed to establish a station near the Comanche Reservation on the Clear Fork of the Brazos, soon named Camp Cooper.

Fort Martin Scott, now decommissioned, served only as a forage station and tenting ground for the Second Cavalry troopers traveling along the old Pinta Trail from Fort Mason to Camp Verde and San Antonio. During this time, Government Crossing in Center Point was a site at which the military road crossed the Guadalupe River (29° 56' 36" N, 99° 01' W).

The Second Cavalry spent five and a half years in Texas, serving out along the hazardous frontier. Davis named Colonel Albert Sidney Johnston the first commander of the Second Cavalry, which was commanded at various times by George H. Thomas, Earl van Dorn and Robert E. Lee. The Second was Lee's last command in the United States Army.[235]

Chapter 17
Civil War

I can anticipate no greater calamity for the country than dissolution of the union. Secession is nothing but revolution.

–Robert E. Lee, 1861

Secession

In 1860, Gillespie County voted 400 to 17 against secession from the Union. In the late winter of 1861, Texas counties sent delegates to a special convention to debate the merits of secession. The state convention adopted an Ordinance of Secession by a vote of 166 to 8, which was ratified by a popular referendum on February 23. Separately from the Ordinance of Secession, Texas also issued a declaration of causes spelling out the rationale for secession. The document specifies several reasons for secession, including its solidarity with its "sister slave-holding States," the Federal government's inability to prevent Indian attacks, slave-stealing raids and other border-crossing acts of banditry. It accuses Northern politicians and abolitionists of a variety of outrages on Texans. The bulk of the document offers a justification of slavery and white supremacy, including this extract:[236]

We hold as undeniable truths that the governments of the various States, and of the confederacy itself, were established exclusively by the white race, for themselves and their posterity; that the African race had no agency in their establishment; that they were rightfully held and regarded as an inferior and dependent race, and in that condition only could their existence in this country be rendered beneficial or tolerable.

During the Civil War, Fort Martin Scott had no strategic position. The old U.S. Army Post did serve as Confederate mustering station, Ranger camp, militia post, forage station and POW camp. It is reported that the Confederate army occupied the post for "intimidation" purposes.[237]

UNIONISTS

Unionists from Kerr, Gillespie and Kendall Counties participated in the formation of the Union League, a secret organization, to support President Abraham Lincoln's policies. German Texans favored the Union because it could better defend the frontier, provide a more enduring condition for economic development and uphold existing social and legal relationships. Texans also supported the Union for less rational motives:[238]

Unionism grew from habit and from the almost religious zeal with which some viewed their country. Memories and shared experiences common to Americans, such as the American Revolution and the War of 1812, perpetuated the habit and contributed to the zeal. Party ideology and point of origin also contributed to this Unionism of the heart. In general Whigs from the Border States and German refugees of the 1848 revolution were among the most persistent Unionists. Close identification with symbols of the nation, such as Sam Houston's affinity for Andrew Jackson, also contributed.[239]

Most of the numerous German pioneers were against leaving the Union, while most of the other residents voted for secession. In 1854, "German Texans declared slavery to be evil."[240] Unionists from Kerr, Gillespie and Kendall Counties were among those who participated in the formation of the Union League in the summer of 1861, and by the summer of 1862, they had formed companies to protect the frontier against Indians and their families against local Confederate forces.

In June 1861, key officials in Gillespie County—the mayor and sheriff of Fredericksburg, the city's leading grocer and butcher and Confederate enrollment officer Kuechler among them—secretly organized as the Union Loyal League.[211]

Jacob Kuechler was authorized to enlist a company of mounted rangers at Fort Martin Scott for frontier defense. The formation of Kuechler's company in February 1862 aggravated Hill Country Confederates anew. Jacob Kuechler signed up only German Unionists in his frontier company and was soon dismissed by Governor Francis R. Lubbock.[212]

In 1862, fifty-four Gillespie county men joined the Confederate army at the Fort Martin Scott mustering station. Eventually, three hundred would enlist with the CSA to avoid conscription.

The Thirty-first Brigade of Texas State Troops was mustered at Fort Martin Scott; Colonel J.M. Norris enrolled two hundred men, including many Germans, placing in command of Ranger companies, among others, Engelbert Krauskopf, Charles Nimitz and William Wahrmund, all leading Fredericksburg men. Units were organized for the defense of the state. As such, they were not considered part of the Confederate army.[213]

Still, the authorities suspected that many of Norris's command had volunteered simply to escape Confederate conscription; included were both Union and Confederate sympathizers. By March 1862, only fifty-four men from Gillespie County had joined the regular Confederate army.

Captain James Duff

On April 28, 1862, General Hamilton Bee succeeded McCulloch as military commandant for south Texas. Bee apparently decided that McCulloch had correctly assessed the situation and immediately declared martial law, posting to Gillespie and Kerr Counties a detachment of Partisan Rangers. Captain James Duff[214] was in command, given authority to do whatever was necessary to end resistance. The martial law order, among several provisions, required all males over sixteen to register with regional provost marshals and take an oath of allegiance, and it declared depreciation (refusal to accept Confederate money) a hostile act. Captain

Duff ordered all men in the Hill Country to report to him within six days and take the required oath, but in the rugged territory north of Kerrville, many neither heard of Duff and his instructions nor, in any event, were inclined to make an arduous trip to comply; accordingly, when approached by Duff's men, they received rough treatment.[245]

Duff declared himself provost and then stated in a letter, "The God damn Dutchmen are Unionists to a man…I will hang all I suspect of being anti-Confederates."[246]

Hangings were, in fact, frequent. Letters from German residents of Fredericksburg attest that many of them would leave their homes at sundown and hide in the surrounding woods in fear of raiding Anglo "guerrillas," or *Hangebund* (or *Die Haengerbaende*, "the hanging band"), who rode up in the night, snatched young men from their beds, hanged their parents and burned their homes for avoiding conscription. Persecution of neutral and pro-Union Germans drove hundreds from their homes—some all the way to Union states, Mexico or even back to Germany.

The notorious James W. Duff was put in charge of Gillespie and Kerr Counties. Captain of an irregular Texas Confederate military unit, "Duff's Partisan Rangers," he arrested Union sympathizers and destroyed their farms. Gillespie County residents took to the hills to escape this reign of terror. Duff's command was later expanded into the Thirty-third Texas.[247]

Among the many local camps from which Duff's troops operated were Camp Pedernales (30° 13.036' N, 99° 0.706' W) at present-day Morris Ranch and Camp Davis (30° 11.702' N, 99° 7.177' W). Captain Henry T. Davis of Duff's "Partisan Rangers" established Camp Davis in 1862. Also operating out of Camp Davis were "minutemen" irregulars under the command of Major James M. Hunter, as well as Captain Duff's forces. Later, a squad from William Quantrill's command arrived here, fresh from Kansas atrocities, led by Bill Paul. They made contact with James P. Waltrip at Fort Martin Scott. Waltrip, emboldened by the Quantrill men, organized his friends and the Quantrill men into the infamous *Hangebund* that conducted terrorist raids throughout the area.[248]

Inquisition by Duff was often savage. To obtain information, his soldiers infrequently resorted to bullwhips; other times, they would hang a person by the neck and then release their victim just before strangulation, repeating the process until either the examination had been completed or the would-be respondent was dead.

A patrol just out of Camp Davis found John Turknette and his grandfather, Jacob Turknette, north of Kerrville looking for lost livestock.

Separating the pair, troopers beat Jacob Turknette to death with bullwhips while others alternately hanged and questioned John Turknette in an effort to get information about his father, Philip Brandon Turknette. The boy died without revealing the location of his father, who subsequently fled to Mexico.

Duff is credited with killing between twenty and fifty men during his second foray into the Hill Country. Some two thousand local residents took to the hills to escape Duff's malice.[249]

Guido Ransleben's 1954 book *A Hundred Years of Comfort in Texas* includes a letter written in 1908 from Howard Henderson to J.W. Sansom that says, in part:

> *I know that J.W. Duff and his company of murderers killed many of my neighbors and friends. My uncle and cousins, Schram Henderson, my wife's father and brother, Turknette, were murdered; my neighbors, Hiram Nelson, Frank Scott and his father, Parson Johnson and old man Scott were all butchered by Duff and his gang. Rocks were tied to their feet and they were thrown into Spring Creek.*[250]

These men, who were beaten and hanged, were tossed into nearby Spring Creek in Gillespie County. Their womenfolk and children buried the victims there. A grim reminder of the incident is a granite monument erected at the mass grave. The spot is known locally as Dead Men's Hole (30° 18' 40" N, 99° 03' 41" W). Their crime was failure to come in and pledge loyalty within three days.

Also among those hanged in this incident was Gus Tegener, brother of Fritz Tegener.[251] The Tegeners were millers and had built and operated a mill near the confluence of Tegener Creek and the Guadalupe River (30° 3.96' N, 99° 19.149' W), just below what is now Schumacher's Crossing in Kerr County. The third Tegener brother, William Tegener, had been hanged by unknown "bandits" in 1857, and his body was thrown over a fifty- to seventy-five-foot bluff into the river below.[252]

The CSA held 215 local men prisoner at Fort Mason in 1862; they were later transferred to Austin. Fort Martin Scott was used as a POW camp for women and children of suspected Unionist families.[253]

In the face of these cruelties, resentment and resistance grew among the Unionists. In 1862, the Union Loyal League met on Bear Creek (approximately 30° 7' N, 98° 57' W). Some five hundred members took part in the rally. Participants raised three companies of Unionist volunteers. Fritz Tegener, Kerr County treasurer, was elected major and took command of the battalion.[254]

Jacob Kuechler, who then barely avoided arrest, immediately disbanded the three Confederate companies. He sent word to the ranks that all persons wanting to make a run for Mexico to escape further conscription should gather at the head of Turtle Creek in Kerr County.[255]

On August 1, 1862, sixty-eight men—sixty-three Germans, one Mexican and four Anglos—answered the call and assembled at the appointed place and time. The troop comprised mostly older men and a few young boys from Mason, Kendall, Kerr and Gillespie Counties, but all of them were targeted conscripts. Kuechler served as a guide for these conscientious objectors attempting to flee to Mexico.[256]

Battle of the Nueces

At Fort Martin Scott, Duff received word of the conscripts' flight and burst into a rage. To Duff, the Germans were simply deserters, and there was but one fate for deserters. Duff sent notice of the "desertions" to First Lieutenant Colin D. McRae and instructed him to intercept the Germans by forced march, at any cost. There is also a great deal of evidence that, even at this early point, Duff let McRae know that he didn't want to hear any word about "survivors" of any conflict that might ensue.[257] Lieutenant McRae was at Camp Pedernales (Morris Ranch) when he received orders from Captain Duff to scout and break up any armed encampments in the area. McRae's command included ninety-four men who were detached from Captain John Donaldson's Company of the Second Texas Mounted Rifles, Duff's Company of Texas Partisan Rangers, Captain Henry T. Davis's Company of Texas State Troops and Major Joseph Taylor's Eighth Texas Cavalry Battalion.[258]

The consequence of Duff's order was the infamous Battle of the Nueces, conversely known as the "Nueces Massacre." Among the conflicting contemporary and eyewitness accounts, the version published in 1905 by the military professional Sansom appears to be the most reliable and complete.[259]

The Texans intercepted the Germans on the west bank of the Nueces River (twenty miles from Fort Clark) on August 10, 1862. In the skirmish, the Confederate forces attacked and killed the majority of the fleeing immigrants.

Unsuspecting, outnumbered and outgunned, about thirty of Tegener's men were killed in the fighting, and twenty were wounded, captured and executed on the spot with a bullet in the back of the head. Six more were killed trying to escape across the Rio Grande. Of the twenty or so escapees who managed to flee for Mexico, seven or eight were killed by yet another patrolling Confederate force in October as they tried to cross the Rio Grande, and nine more were captured at various locations and executed out of hand.[260]

LOYAL TO THE UNION

On August 10, 1865, exactly three years after the Battle of the Nueces, Harry Schwethelm[261] led a group from Comfort to the battle site to retrieve the bones of his fallen comrades. They brought the bones back to Comfort and buried them in a mass grave (29° 58.204' N, 98° 54.313' W). Next to the grave, the residents of Comfort erected a tall limestone obelisk as a monument to the German men and boys killed during the battle. Inscribed on the east face of the monument are the words "Treue der Union" ("Loyal to the Union"). There is a Texas Historical Marker,[262] and the site is listed on the National Register of Historic Places.[263]

Treue der Union. *Photo by Joseph Luther, 2009.*

The Treue der Union monument was dedicated on August 10, 1866, in Kendall County. The obelisk stands twenty feet high and was constructed of native limestone by local stonemasons and several carvers. The main obelisk weighs 35,700 pounds, with the top containing the original four name tablets. The United States flag has thirty-six stars, representing the number of states at the time of the monument dedication. On the lawn at the base are four name tablets in German. Inside the second course of the monument is a time capsule. It is the only German-language monument to the Union in the South where the remains of those killed in battle are buried, as well as where an 1866 thirty-six-star American flag flies at half-staff.[264]

FRONTIER REGIMENT

In the spring of 1864, Company A of the Frontier Regiment, under William Banta,[265] attempted to enforce the law when a series of murders, robberies and outrages perpetrated by bushwhackers, state troops of the Third Frontier District and men of the Frontier Regiment excited the populace of Gillespie and Kendall Counties into a frenzy. Banta's participation in the arrest and execution of an outlaw in Gillespie County led to his arrest. He and six other men were incarcerated in Fredericksburg.[266]

Major James Hunter, commander of state troops of the Third Frontier District, wrote to Governor Pendleton Murrah and requested that he be allowed to send the men to prison in Austin or San Antonio. Shortly afterward, an armed group of more than two hundred men rode into Fredericksburg and overcame the twelve-man guard stationed at the jail. They pushed their way into the stone jail and opened fire on the prisoners, who were located in two small rooms separated by a hallway. They killed one of the prisoners instantly and critically wounded four others, two of whom died the next day. Banta survived the episode but was badly wounded in both legs.[267]

The Mounted Regiment, Texas State Troops, was transferred into the Confederate army on March 1, 1864. The transfer spelled the effective end of Texas's Frontier Regiment. Fort Martin Scott is said to have been occupied by the Confederate forces from 1961 to 1865,[268] but it is not listed as an official post for the Texas State Troops, although the records of Camp Davis are among the adjutant general's Texas State Troops Records at the Texas State Archives. Fredericksburg is recorded as the site of the Percussion Cap Factory[269] and headquarters for the Second and Third Frontier Districts.[270]

On March 31, 1864, several anxious families of Gillespie, Kerr and Kendall Counties—already victimized by both jayhawkers[271] and Indians—"forted up" together in common defense. Upon hearing that Company "A" at Camp Davis in Gillespie County had been order redeployed, they petitioned the adjutant general to block the move.[272] They were unsuccessful. On April 11, 1864, Captain James E. McCord himself was ordered to concentrate what was left of his regiment in Austin and then to proceed with it to Anderson in Grimes County in east Texas. Challenged by two simultaneous wars, the frontier settlers within a few short weeks were conjoined with and then abandoned by the Confederacy.[273]

WAR'S END

At the end of the war, nearly five thousand Texans had deserted from Confederate and state service. Formal order had disappeared into lawlessness in many areas of Texas. Local minutemen and vigilantes patrolled the county and stood guard along the old Pinta Trail. Their duty was to intercept brigands, rustlers, fugitives and hell-raisers who were taking advantage of the breakdown of law and order in this rough area. The number of outlaws in Gillespie County swelled to hundreds. Most outlaws were army veterans, proficient, well-armed and wretched gunmen of the outlaw Josey Wales sort.[274]

The Comanche, Kiowa, Lipan Apache and Kickapoo Indian nations were determined to retain the lands they had taken back during the Civil War. The Indian tribes had become aggressive during the absence of military forces from the Hill Country during the war. Hostile Indian warriors pushed back the frontier fifty miles or more. There is no question that settlers suffered greatly, having perhaps four hundred men, women and children killed, wounded or carried off along the edge of western civilization in Texas.[275] The frontier west of the Gainesville/Fredericksburg/Kerrville line was abandoned by all but a few brave people, who moved into stockades. "The worst raids were on moonlit nights, and the soft summer moon became a harbinger of death."[276]

Chapter 18
Fourth United States Cavalry

Clean up the mess in Texas.
–President Ulysses S. Grant to Major General Philip Sheridan

After the Civil War, Grant ordered Major General Philip Sheridan to Texas with fifty thousand soldiers to threaten the French-sponsored regime of Emperor Ferdinand Maximilian Joseph in Mexico. For more than a year, Sheridan tried to persuade the French to leave Mexico. Sheridan was also tasked to deal with the Texas Indians and outlaws. Ultimately, it was the Indians who would be the greatest threat.

Comanche, Kiowas, Lipan Apaches and Kickapoos controlled the Hill Country above the Balcones Escarpment. Sheridan ordered the Fourth U.S. Cavalry into Texas in 1866 to combat these tough adversaries. The regiment was filled with skilled Civil War veterans from both armies and outfitted with the latest and best equipment. In War Department records of that day, the Fourth Cavalry was rated the best cavalry regiment in the U.S. Army. Ten companies were concentrated at San Antonio, and two companies were sent to the Rio Grande. In the fall of 1866, companies were sent to Camp Verde, old Fort Martin Scott at Fredericksburg and Fort Mason. The Fourth U.S. Cavalry arrived at Fort Martin Scott in September 1866, taking three months to stop Indian raids.[277]

The Fourth U.S. Cavalry reactivated Fort Martin Scott in September 1866 for only a few months. The conditions of the old army post at that time are unclear but were apparently sufficient for it to serve as a garrison for the

General Philip Sheridan. *Photo by Matthew Brady.*

Fourth. An 1855 newspaper advertisement offered the site for sale to include a number of houses, stables and more to accommodate a regiment of soldiers.[278]

The Indian Wars in Texas created quite a reputation for General Sheridan. During his lifetime, Sheridan was known as a fierce enemy of the Indians, and his approach to the Indians was encapsulated in the saying, "The only good Indian is a dead Indian," although he himself denied having said this when criticized by his political opponents. Sheridan also outraged locals when he was quoted as saying, "If I owned hell and Texas, I would rent out Texas and live in hell."[279]

After leading the campaigns into Indian Territory to stop hostile tribes from raiding border settlements in Texas and Kansas, Sheridan established Fort Sill, Oklahoma, on January 8, 1869. This became the reservation of the banished Texas Indians.

For years following the Civil War, Gillespie County continued to contend with the political, social, cultural and economic troubles produced by the war. By the end of the war, nearly five thousand Texans had deserted from Confederate and state service, and an unknown number had avoided conscription.[280] Many became desperados, outlaws, rustlers and gun hands. Gunfights proliferated. In Kerrville, seventeen outlaws tried to rob the Schreiner mercantile, and a shootout occurred downtown. Five outlaws were shot down in the street, and the rest were hunted down.[281]

In the field, at Fort Martin Scott, a Fourth Cavalry trooper was given much latitude in the uniform he wore. The nonregulation cowboy hat was much preferred to the forage cap. Field coats were seldom worn, and long-sleeve shirts were common. Troopers were armed with Model 1865 Springfield Trapdoor carbine with sling; the rifle cartridge was designated as .45-70-405, indicating a .45 caliber with a 405-grain bullet propelled by 70 grains of black powder. It had a muzzle velocity of 1,350 feet per second, making it a powerful load. There was also the Colt Model 1860 .44 cartridge revolver; it had a six-shot, rotating cylinder and fired a 0.454-inch-diameter (11.5 millimeter) round lead ball, or a conical projectile, that was propelled by a 30-grain charge of black powder ignited by a copper percussion cap that contained a volatile charge of fulminate of mercury (a substance that explodes upon impact). The percussion cap, when struck by the hammer, ignited the powder charge. When fired, balls had a muzzle velocity of about 900 feet per second.

Troopers carried about one hundred rounds of rifle and ten rounds of pistol ammunition. The men also carried a Model 1860 cavalry saber and a belt knife. There was a lariat and picket pin to tether his horse. He rode an 1859 McClellan saddle.

Patrol staple articles of food were coffee, bacon and hard bread. Often, when conditions such as the proximity of the enemy permitted, fresh meat was obtained by hunting. This consisted of buffalo, venison and smaller game, which generally abounded on the frontier.

Reports for the Fifth Military District in Texas indicate that patrols of the Fourth Cavalry against the Comanches in the Hill Country often exceeded six hundred miles.[282]

By December 1866, Fort Martin Scott had been permanently abandoned by military units. The Fourth Cavalry concentrated in garrisons in a few large posts, including San Antonio, Fort Concho, Fort Duncan, Fort Griffin, Fort McKavett and Fort Clark. Fort Clark was reoccupied by the Fourth Cavalry in 1866. It was the base of Colonel Ranald S. ("Bad Hand") Mackenzie and his Fourth Cavalry in many operations against the Lipans, Comanches and Kickapoos in the Indian Wars of the 1870s.[283]

The Fourth Cavalry went to on fame and glory, defeating the Mexican Kickapoos and Quanah Parker's Comanches.[284] This fabled army unit, under the command of Colonel Mackenzie, became the basis for the unit in John Wayne movie *Rio Grande*.[285]

CHAPTER 19
BRAEUTIGAM GARDENS

Mr. Braeutigam, who was a courageous man, reached for his musket which was standing in the corner when the robber's bullet struck him fatally.
—"The Murder of John W. Braeutigam," 1890

Johann Wolfgang Braeutigam, his wife, Christine, and their nine children eventually settled in Fredericksburg. In 1870, the family moved into the abandoned Fort Martin Scott, from which Braeutigam operated a biergarten.

The Braeutigam Farm was part of Survey 36, which was patented by the Republic of Texas to Nathaniel Townsend, as assignee of W.O. Merriwether, on December 6, 1845. Townsend sold the 640-acre parcel for one dollar per acre to John Twohig on February 2, 1852. John Twohig sold an undivided half interest in the survey to J.J.B. Wright, who was a doctor in the United States Army. Braeutigam's Farm was also part of Survey 34, located by Certificate No. 43 issued to Jose Soto and patented to John Twohig, assignee by patent No. 230, Vol. 4, dated January 23, 1847.[286]

The old Fort Martin Scott buildings were scavenged and salvaged by locals seeking building materials for use in construction. When Braeutigam purchased the land in 1870, only the officers' quarters and the large rock stable remained.

The Braeutigam family renovated the former officers' quarters into a home. They also built a small store and saloon near the road to San Antonio—the old Pinta Trail. To this, Mr. Braeutigam added a grapevine arbor and planted cedars, hackberries and other native shrubs and trees. The place became well known as Braeutigam Gardens.

Braeutigam's Farm. *Gillespie County Historical Society.*

In 1883, the first Gillespie County Fair was held east of Fredericksburg on what had once been Fort Martin Scott. The site had been purchased by John W. Braeutigam in 1870 after the Civil War, and became "Braeutigam's Garden," a dance hall. The abandoned fort parade grounds were dragged by logs for use as the first racetrack. County fairs and Fourth of July and Easter celebrations were held at Braeutigam Gardens.[287]

Here at Braeutigam's Garden, on September 3, 1884, Braeutigam was murdered by four strangers in a robbery of the biergarten's cashbox:

> *Mr. Wolfgang Braeutigam, or John Braeutigam...was a well-liked person and was about 55 years of age at the time of his unfortunate experience. On September 3, 1884, four strangers entered his establishment and asked for some drinks. When he served them the drinks, one of the men drew his revolver and sought to empty the money chest. Mr. Braeutigam, who was a courageous man, reached for his musket which was standing in the corner when the robber's bullet struck him fatally. The money till contained only a small sum.*
>
> *Since the business establishment was located some distance from the nearest residences, it enabled the perpetrators to escape unmolested. One*

> *of them was shot by a ranger in the lower country when he resisted arrest. Another was delivered to the local jail and met with death when the jail was destroyed by fire. A few years later, the third one was shot to death above Mason, and the fourth one, presumably the one who committed the murder, a fellow named Fannin, escaped.*[288]

Owned from 1870 by members of the Braeutigam family, Fort Martin Scott was sold to the City of Fredericksburg in 1959. In 1986, the Fredericksburg Heritage Federation began the extensive work of reconstructing the site as a tourist attraction.[289] Among highlights of the fort are the post commander's quarters (formerly Braeutigam Garden), six buildings of officers' housing, a sutler's store and warehouse, a laundry, a bake house with oven, a military hospital, three sets of enlisted men's barracks, a quartermaster's warehouse, a stable with barn and a blacksmith shop. The guardhouse, made of cut limestone, is the only surviving building from the original fort, having been restored to its original design in the early 1990s. It was also the Braeutigam homestead.[290]

Chapter 20
Tomorrow Isn't What It Was Yesterday

Give us a country we can call our own, where we can bury our people in quiet.
–Katemcy

Penateka chief Katemcy was the first to discuss the possibility of moving onto a reservation. In May 1850, Katemcy complained to the Indian agent Judge John H. Rollins that the Penatekas were starving due to lack of game. Katemcy suggested that his band of three hundred Comanches might be willing to abandon raiding and hunting and learn to farm. In 1851, Katemcy met with Indian agent John A. Rogers and stated that his people had been "driven from their homes where their parents were buried…by the white men and have no home or resting place. We want land and homes of our own." If only the president would give his tribe a section of the country "to settle on and cultivate that we can call our own," his band of Penatekas would gladly move there and live under the protection of the federal government. Of course, Rogers was powerless to act, as the Texas legislature refused any land for the Indians.[291]

In 1852, Katemcy was found "very much in want" at his encampment on the headwaters of the San Sabá River. The Penateka chief rode with thirty tribesmen to Fort Martin Scott to obtain some food. This entry into Fredericksburg was not the glorious procession of 1847.

Essentially hat in hand, Katemcy restated his band's desire to move to a reservation and raise crops. He then took his people to live among Sanaco's people on the Concho River. By September 1852, both bands—some seven hundred individuals—were "suffering extreme hunger, bordering on starvation."

The two Penateka chiefs met with Indian agent Horace Capron at Camp J.E. Johnson on the North Concho River, fifteen miles northwest of present-day San Angelo:[292]

> *How* [could we] *attempt the cultivation of the soil, or raising of cattle, so long as we have no permanent home?...Over this vast country, where for centuries our ancestors roamed in undisputed possession, free and happy, what have we left? The game, our main dependence, is killed and driven off and we are forced into the most sterile and barren portions of it to starve...Give us a country we can call our own, where we can bury our people in quiet.*[293]

By 1853, all four Penateka bands—those of Katemcy, Sanaco, Buffalo Hump and Saviah—were at Fort Chadbourne to receive food. They were starving. Late that same year, President Franklin Pierce, Secretary of War Jefferson Davis and the reappointed Indian agent Robert S. Neighbors pressured Governor Peter Hansbrough Bell—former commander of the Texas Rangers—to provide for the establishment of federally supervised Indian reservations in Texas. Twelve leagues (53,136 acres) of vacant land were placed under federal government jurisdiction "for the use and benefit of the several tribes of Indians residing within the limits of Texas."[294]

The Brazos Reserve,[295] just below present-day Graham, became home to Caddo, Waco, Anadarko and Tonkawa tribes. On the Clear Fork of the Brazos in Throckmorton County, Penateka Comanches lived on the 18,576-acre Comanche Reserve.[296] This smaller reservation contained four hundred souls—all Comanches, known as the Southern band of that tribe. Their head chief was known by the name of Ketemesie (Katemcy).[297] The federal Indian agent in charge of both reservations was Major Robert S. Neighbors. The U.S. Army established Camp Cooper[298] in 1856 to keep watch over and protect the adjacent Comanche Indian Reservation.

During the years the reservations struggled to survive, central Texas gradually was being settled by Anglo-Americans, who failed to distinguish between the reservation Comanches and the nonreservation Comanches. The latter continued to raid in Texas and Mexico, and their raids angered settlers, providing a rationalization for legislative action to encourage their removal from Texas. By 1858, the Penateka Comanches on the reservation were being harassed by nonreservation Comanches and their allies, the Kiowas, a situation that made life even more difficult for residents of the reservation.[299]

By 1859, Neighbors and his two Indian agents had bowed to the difficulty of protecting the tribes settled on the Lower Reserve. A letter to Neighbors from Matthew Leeper, the Indian agent on the Comanche Reservation, summarized the concerns:

> *The more familiar I become of the wants and necessities of these people* [Penateka Comanches] *the more thoroughly I am convinced of the propriety and justice of your* [Neighbors's] *conclusion repeatedly and long since expressed in reference to them, that the only appropriate place for them to settle and learn the arts of civilization was upon Indian Territory near the Wichita Mountains, where they would have a country to roam over at will upon which to herd and collect their animals and other goods.*[300]

Only a small group of Comanches, elements of the Penateka band, came to the reservation, while their kinsmen continued to live freely and aggressively raid the frontier. The reservation plan might have worked had the area not filled up with white settlers almost immediately. Since the whites established horse and cattle ranches, the area naturally became a target for Comanche, Kiowa and Kickapoo raids; whites believed that the proximity of the reservations had something to do with the raids and blamed the reservation population for either conducting or abetting them. There may be some justification for accusing the reservation Comanches, since they entertained nonreservation Comanche visitors and their social structure could not prevent young men from leaving the reservation to live with other bands.[301]

A number of racist and violence-prone Anglos in the region, led by the incendiary former Indian agent John Robert Baylor,[302] favored either Indian extermination or removal and opposed all assimilation efforts. While serving as Indian agent at the Comanche Reserve on the Clear Fork beginning in September 1855, Baylor became convinced that some of the reservations Indians were committing depredations in neighboring counties and then returning to the safety of the reservation. Baylor found himself out of work by May 1857. Fired for misuse of federal funds and having lost the confidence of the reserve Indians, Baylor blamed the federal superintendent of the reservations, Robert S. Neighbors, for his termination.[303]

On May 23, 1859, Baylor and 250 men (including cattle rancher Charles Goodnight)[304] attacked the Brazos Reservation, south of present-day Graham, killing five, including two elderly Indians. Residents of Belknap told Neighbors that Baylor's attacking party included some unsavory types, specifically "fifty horse thieves and well-known desperados." The Indian superintendent said that these outlaws were "stealing horses from the reserves, and from the citizens around it, waylaying roads, stopping travelers, robbing wagons, and stopping the mails."

Texas governor Hardin Richard Runnels refused to help, claiming that the matter was the jurisdiction of the U.S. Eighth Military District. Texas Ranger captain John "Rip" Ford protested in a letter to President James Buchanan's Indian commissioner that "I have never been able to detect the Reserve Indians in the commission of a single depredation…and I do think the measures instituted by the people [Baylor and his group] have been impolitic and precipitate."

Robert S. Neighbors, unable to adequately protect his charges and wanting to avoid their mass slaughter at the hands of whites, hurriedly relocated all of the reservation Indians. In August 1859, protected by three companies of federal troops under Major George Thomas, Neighbors personally led his charges to safety across the Red River into Indian Territory in what is now modern Oklahoma.[305]

Ernest Wallace, west Texas teacher and historian, recorded this as a long, strange and colorful procession of Indians out of the Brazos Reservations, never to return. The sight was at once magnificent and pathetic. There were 384 Comanches and 1,112 Indians from other tribes."[306]

Robert S. Neighbors reported, "Reflecting on the numerous violent and lawless events over the previous nine months, I have this day crossed all the Indians out of the heathen land of 'Texas' and am now out of the land of the philistines."[307]

On September 14, 1859, at the county seat of Belknap, Major Robert S. Neighbors was assassinated—blasted with a shotgun in the back by Edward Cornett, one of Baylor's gang of vigilantes. In a letter to his father, David G. Burnet, Lieutenant William Burnet wrote, "The 'Baylor Party' have murdered Major Neighbors…the assassination…was a most foul and cowardly murder."[308]

These reservations were closed in 1859. In 1870, the Lipan Apache Band of Texas resided at Fort Griffin, Texas, with twenty-six tribal members. In 1905, the Lipan Apache Band of Texas resided on the Mescalero Indian Reservation in New Mexico, with an estimated number of between twenty and forty tribal members. Today, the only Indians remaining in Texas are located on the Alabama-Coushatta Indian Reservation, just east of Houston, and the two other tribes—the Tiguas and the Kickapoos—both live in the valley of the Rio Grande.

Chapter 21
A Fort of Reason

Conclusions arrived at through reasoning have very little or no influence in altering the course of our lives.

—*Carlos Castenada*

Fort Martin Scott still stands today, or at least some parts of it. It is a museum and a rare opportunity to explore a relic of the Texas Indian Wars. Over the years, reenactors have fought skirmishes here, Comanches have staged powwows and flint knappers have convened "knap ins" on the old parade grounds. They come for the history and the revelations of heritage. It is a spiritual landscape. Fort Martin Scott exists today because of the Pinta Trail, which was created more than ten thousand years ago. The Lipan Apache and Penateka Comanche bands claimed this Hill Country as their homeland. The Spanish trekked by on this path to establish missions and subdue the various tribes and bands, creating the Presidio San Luis de las Amarillas and the nearby Santa Cruz de San Sabá Mission. The fabled Los Almagres silver mines and Jim Bowie's lost silver mine attracted the German Adelsverein.

As German immigrants began to move westward along the Pinta Trail, the Republic of Texas went to war against the hostile Indians. The Texas Rangers in the 1830s and 1840s patrolled this region. Battles were fought and legends were created. The German immigrants came to this area full of promise and hope. To achieve this dream, they signed a lasting treaty with the Penateka Comanches; the troops at Fort Martin Scott were given the responsibility, but not the authority, to guard this treaty.

When Texas became part of the United States, the U.S. Army was given the responsibility for peacekeeping and humanitarian services for all peoples of the Hill Country. Fort Martin Scott was the result. It had one purpose: to serve and protect.

Many famous American heroes served at Fort Martin Scott. These grounds were walked by men like General James Longstreet, General Robert E. Lee, Brigadier General Seth Eastman, Jesse Chisholm, General St. George Cooke, General Richard Irving Dodge, Captain James W. Duff, General Ranald S. Mackenzie, Indian agent Robert S. Neighbors, Texas Ranger John Coffee Hays and Penateka chiefs including Katemcy, Buffalo Hump, Santa Anna and Old Owl, as well as Lipan Apache chiefs such as Flacco, Castro and Chiquito.

Fort Martin Scott is an opportunity to preserve and impart our shared heritage for all time. This special place is a resource and a treasure.

FORT MARTIN SCOTT

Sit a spell with me
Under the live oak tree
Read all these old tales
And listen and see.

Close by the Pinta Trail,
The old Fort stands.
Parade the grounds,
Stand the guard.

Hear the bugle call,
Feel the thunderous hoofs
As the fancy Dragoons
Sortie forth flags and all.

Comanches, Apaches,
Rangers and Soldiers
Dashing about in lethal battle
Attack one day and dance the next.

They are all gone to ground now.
All that is left are the
Memories and myths of
Old Fort Martin Scott.

Appendix

Archaeological Investigations

Fort Martin Scott was nominated for the National Register of Historic Places by E.E. Prewitt in 1979.[309]

The first archaeological testing was conducted at Fort Martin Scott by the Center for Archaeological Research—University of Texas at San Antonio (CAR-UTSA)[310] in 1983. Wagner and Klein Inc. prepared a "Preservation Plan" for the Fort Martin Scott property and buildings.

Formal archaeological fieldwork was commenced at Fort Martin Scott in 1986. The fort is a record Texas Archaeological Site, #41GL52. Between May 24 and 30, 1986, the University of Texas–San Antonio was engaged by the Fredericksburg Heritage Federation "to locate and map as many buildings of the original fort as possible." The project was conducted under the general supervision of Thomas R. Hester (principal investigator) and Jack D. Eaton. Anne Fox was the project director and co-principal investigator. Joseph Labadie was the project field director and author.[311]

Subsequent investigations were undertaken in 1988, 1989, 1990, 1991, 1993, 1996, 1999, 2001, 2010 and 2012. Structures were identified, and an intensive survey was performed within the confines of the original 11.2-acre army post.[312]

Research and field methods employed during the 1986 followed the Council of Texas Archaeologists' performance guidelines and consisted of standard field recording procedures. All extant building foundations were mapped by plane table and alidade.[313]

The CAR-UTSA fieldwork in 1983 resulted in identification and test excavations at eight different structural remains. Three additional areas were

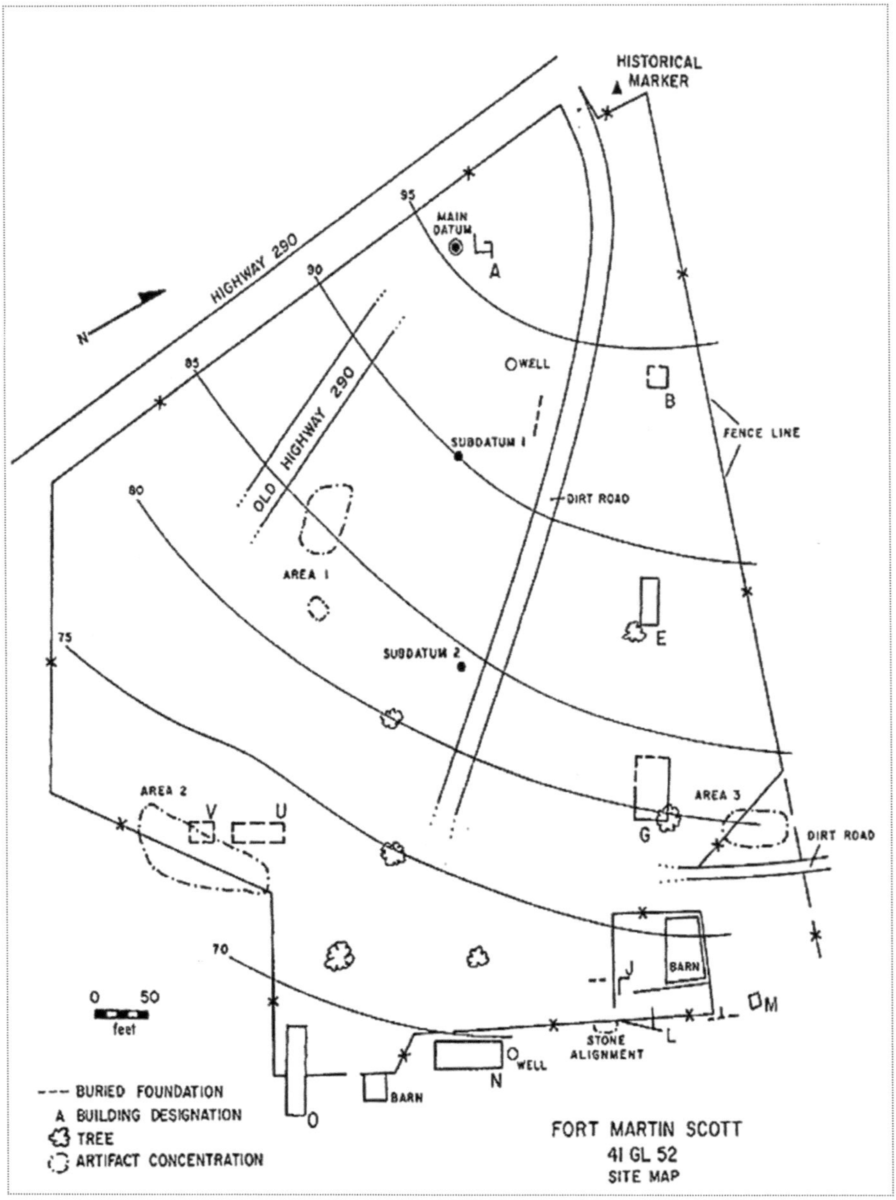

Archaeological survey map. *Archaeological Investigation at Fort Martin Scott (41GL52) in Gillespie County, Texas.*

intensively surveyed but did not result in the identification of foundation remains.[311] The eleven specific sites follow.

Post Commander's Residence—Structure A

This building is located on the west side of the former parade ground and within about 100 feet of the present U.S. 290 roadbed. The 1853 Freeman Report describes this structure as a log building with four rooms 15x17 feet in dimensions, with porches front and rear. The only remaining indications of this structure consist of a few scattered limestone rocks and a short section of a stone wall. The front of this structure would have faced east toward the parade ground. Few artifacts were recovered from this site and consisted of square nails, broken glass and animal bones. It is noted that this area was the location for "Braeutigam's Garden" of the 1880s.

Officers' Quarters—Structure B

This site is the westernmost structure in the north row of officers' quarters. The Freeman Report describes this building as adobe, two rooms, 10x12 feet, with porches front and rear. The structure faced the parade ground. There were a few scattered rocks on the ground to indicate the general vicinity of this building. A total of seventy-five artifacts was recovered from the ground surface and archaeological testing. These materials included tin can scraps, window glass, a button, two clay pipe fragments and twenty-nine square-cut nails.

Officers' Quarters—Structure E

This site is in the north row of the officers' dwellings. The 1853 Freeman Report describes this structure as adobe with two rooms, 14x16 feet in dimension, with porches front and rear. The building faced the parade ground. During the initial surface survey, a total of thirty artifacts was collected. These included fifteen square-cut nails, two undecorated whiteware sherds and a few window glass fragments. The archaeological testing of Structure E produced no artifacts.

OFFICERS' QUARTERS—STRUCTURE G

This is the easternmost structure in the north row of officers' quarters. The Freeman Report described this building as adobe, four rooms with a basement, and 166x17 feet in dimension. There was no mention of porches. About 75 percent of the foundation was exposed prior to archaeological testing. A total of twenty-three artifacts was recovered, eighteen of which were found in subsurface contexts.

SUTLER'S STORE—STRUCTURES H AND J

The sutler's store[315] was located in the northeast corner of the parade ground in the vicinity of the weather-boarded barn. The barn was constructed by a member of the Braeutigam family sometime after 1884. Remnants for Structure H are thought to be inside the barn. Subsurface investigation failed to produce a single artifact.

LAUNDRESS' QUARTERS—STRUCTURE L

The Freeman Report of 1853 indicates that this structure was located on the bank of Baron's Creek near the sutler's store and bake house. It was described as constructed of log, 20x14 feet, and contained a storeroom and quarters for the laundry workers. No artifacts were found in the vicinity.

BAKE HOUSE—STRUCTURE M

This building was located adjacent to Barons Creek and 50 feet south of the northeast corner of the property leased to the City of Fredericksburg Heritage Federation (1987). Freeman described this building as a log structure, 14x20 feet. The only remaining evidence of this structure in 1987 was the remains of the foundation for a cut-stone bake oven. Artifacts recovered included ceramic sherds, tin scraps and square-cut nails.

ENLISTED QUARTERS—STRUCTURE O

This building was located at the southeast corner of the parade ground. It was one of two structure (O and P) designated as enlisted quarters. This building was of sufficient size to accommodate one company of soldiers. The Freeman Report described both of these structures as constructed of logs, 46x16 feet, each with three rooms plus a single room. A total of 126 artifacts was recovered.

SURVEY AREA 1—STRUCTURES R AND S

Survey Area 1 corresponds to the location for the enlisted quarters on the south side of the parade ground. Intensive surface survey isolated three discrete clusters of artifacts within the larger area designated as Survey Area 2. A total of nineteen square-cut nails, two pipe fragments, two buttons, one cartridge case and several glass fragments was found randomly scattered across the area. A second small concentration of artifacts was isolated in the western half of Survey Area 1: several square-cut nails, .36-caliber and .44-caliber lead balls, a U.S. military button and two percussion caps for use on military muskets. A third surface scatter was found in Area T. A total of sixty-four square-cut nails and three glass fragments was found in this area.

SURVEY AREA 2—STRUCTURES U AND V

These are the southernmost buildings shown on the 1853 Freeman map. Structure U was the storehouse and was described as consisting of three rooms and an office constructed of log, 14x16 feet. Structure V was the blacksmith shop, constructed of adobe, 14x16 feet. Subsurface testing was not performed in this 1987 investigation. Although metal detector scans indicated fifty-one signals, no artifacts were recovered from this general area.

SURVEY AREA 3—STRUCTURE K

This was the hospital. Freeman described the building as being 12x25 feet in dimension and constructed of untreated logs that were "fast decaying." The location is indicated as being north of Structure G. Intensive surface survey of the general area recovered a total of forty-four historic and prehistoric artifacts. There were no artifacts recovered that would suggest a strictly medical function. Dr. Swift, the post surgeon, had much to say about this facility.[316]

ARCHAEOLOGICAL INVESTIGATION OF THE PROPOSED SITE OF THE FORMER TEXAS RANGER MUSEUM

This study, conducted in January 2012, revealed that the proposed museum would not impinge on the historic buildings and features of the Fort Martin Scott site. The Former Texas Ranger project does occur within the boundaries of the National Register District and the State Archaeological Landmark District.

The 2012 survey recovered 14 historic and 143 prehistoric artifacts. These were recorded as a southern extension of 41GL52 rather than as a new site. The historic artifacts consisted of three .66-caliber round lead balls, three pieces of fired lead shot, a .22-caliber short cartridge case, two .44-caliber rimfire cartridge cases, a shotgun shell base, a barrel band, a saddle cinch ring and a U.S. military general service button.

The prehistoric component of the south end of 41GL52 is a multicomponent campsite and lithic scatter. Recovered artifacts included Ensor and Scallorn points.

The Texas Historic Commission approved this project on January 12, 2012.

Notes

Introduction

1. Paul R.M. Brooks Jr., "Fort Martin Scott," *Handbook of Texas Online*, www.tshaonline.org/handbook/online/articles/qbf33.
2. An excellent sculpture commentating the treaty is located here near the Vereins Kirche Museum on the Marketplatz in Fredericksburg.
3. Otto W. Tetzlaff, "Meusebach-Comanche Treaty," *Handbook of Texas Online*, www.tshaonline.org/handbook/online/articles/mgm01; Biesele, *History of the German Settlements*.
4. Corker and Humphrey, "Texas Frontier in 1850."
5. National Register Reference #80004121.
6. Texas State Historical Marker #10039.
7. Texas State Archaeological Landmark 41GL52. State Archaeological Landmarks are designated by the Texas Historical Commission (THC) and receive legal protection under the *Antiquities Code of Texas*. State Archaeological Landmark designation stipulates that the property cannot be removed, altered, damaged, salvaged or excavated without a permit from the THC.

CHAPTER 1

8. Texas State Historic Marker #10096.
9. Paleo-Indians, or Paleoamericans, is a classification term given to the first peoples who entered, and subsequently inhabited, the American continents during the final glacial episodes of the late Pleistocene period.
10. The gold seekers inevitably came to be called the "Argonauts," after the classic Greek tales of Jason and the Argonauts (seekers of the Golden Fleece).
11. See a page from *Texas Almanac for 1947–48*, Portal to Texas History, http://texashistory.unt.edu/ark:/67531/metapth117136/m1/291.
12. See Texas Beyond History, "Pavo Real," www.texasbeyondhistory.net/pavoreal/index.html.
13. Nina L. Nixon, "Pinta Trail," *Handbook of Texas Online*, www.tshaonline.org/handbook/online/articles/ayp02.
14. Kathleen Kirk Gilmore, "San Luis De Las Amarillas Presidio," *Handbook of Texas Online*, www.tshaonline.org/handbook/online/articles/uqs28.
15. See Texas Beyond History, "Presidio San Saba," www.texasbeyondhistory.net/presidio/index.html.
16. See Texas Beyond History, "Los Almagres, the Lost Spanish Mine," www.texasbeyondhistory.net/plateaus/images/he13.html; Chipman and Weddle, "How Historical Myths Are Born."
17. Ferdinand von Roemer, scientist, traveled to Texas in 1845. From November 1845 to May 8, 1847, he explored from Galveston to Houston, as far west as New Braunfels and Fredericksburg and as far north as Waco, studying the fauna, the flora and the geology of the country.
18. Roemer, *Texas, with Particular Reference*, 247.
19. Prince Karl (or Carl) of Solms-Braunfels (July 27, 1812–November 13, 1875) was a German prince and military officer in both the Austrian army and the cavalry of the Grand Duchy of Hesse. As commissioner general of the Adelsverein, he spearheaded the establishment of colonies of German immigrants in Texas. Prince Solms named New Braunfels, Texas, in honor of his homeland.
20. See Texas Hill Country, "The New Promised Land," www.texfiles.com/enchantedrocktexas/enchantedrockhistory/part_six.htm.
21. Williams, *Old Texas Trails*.

CHAPTER 2

22. S.C. Gwynne quoted in David Bianculli and Terry Gross, "The Rise and Fall of the Comanche Empire," *Fresh Air*, National Public Radio, www.npr.org/2011/05/20/136438816/the-rise-and-fall-of-the-comanche-empire.
23. Fehrenbach, *Comanches: The Destruction of a People.*
24. George Klos, "Comanche Indians," extract from *Handbook of Texas Online*, www.tshaonline.org/tools/article_extracts/bzi4_comanche.html.
25. Art Leatherwood, "Llano Estacado," *Handbook of Texas Online*, www.tshaonline.org/handbook/online/articles/ryl02.
26. Fehrenbach, *Lone Star*, 34.
27. See Wikipedia, "Comanche," http://en.wikipedia.org/wiki/Comanche.
28. Hämäläinen, *Comanche Empire.*
29. Burnet, "Comanches and Other Tribes of Texas."
30. Betty, *Comanche Society*, 68–69.
31. Gwynne, *Empire of the Summer Moon.*
32. Fehrenbach, *Comanches: The History of a People.*
33. Fehrenbach, *Comanches: The History of a People.*
34. Hämäläinen, *Comanche Empire.*
35. Randolph B. Campbell, *Gone to Texas*, 63.
36. Catlin, *North American Indians.*
37. Betty, *Comanche Society*, 87.
38. Fehrenbach, *Comanches: The Destruction of a People*, 305.
39. Ibid., 315.
40. Dixon, *Life of Billy Dixon.*
41. Fehrenbach, *Comanches: The Destruction of a People*, 124.
42. Hunter, *Boy Captives*, 166.
43. Texas Historical Marker #16676.
44. Jodye Lynn Dickson Schilz, "Council House Fight," *Handbook of Texas Online*, www.tshaonline.org/handbook/online/articles/btc01; Webb, *Texas Rangers.*
45. Richardson, *Comanche Barrier*; see Wikipedia, "Battle of Plum Creek." http://en.wikipedia.org/wiki/Battle_of_Plum_Creek.
46. Sam Houston was first commanding general of the Army of the Republic of Texas.
47. Carol A. Lipscomb, "Comanche Indians," *Handbook of Texas Online*, www.tshaonline.org/handbook/online/articles/bmc72.
48. George Klos, "Indians During Statehood," extract from *Handbook of Texas Online*, www.tshaonline.org/tools/article_extracts/bzi4_statehood.html.

49. Gwynne, *Empire of the Summer Moon*, 113.
50. Klos, "Indians during Statehood," extract from *Handbook*.

CHAPTER 3

51. Fehrenbach, *Comanches: The Destruction of a People*.
52. Jodye Lynn Dickson Schilz, "Buffalo Hump," *Handbook of Texas Online*, www.tshaonline.org/handbook/online/articles/fbu12.
53. Marie Giles, "Tehuacana Creek Councils," *Handbook of Texas Online*, www.tshaonline.org/handbook/online/articles/mgt01.
54. Fehrenbach, *Comanches: The Destruction of a People*.
55. Kappler, "Treaty with the Comanche, Aionai, Anadarko, Caddo, Etc., 1846," *Indian Affairs*, vol. 2.
56. Schilz, "Council House Fight," *Handbook*.
57. Brice, *Great Comanche Raid*.
58. See Wikipedia, "Buffalo Hump," http://en.wikipedia.org/wiki/Buffalo_Hump.
59. Ibid.
60. Jodye Lynn Dickson Schilz, "Santa Anna," *Handbook of Texas Online*, www.tshaonline.org/handbook/online/articles/fsa30.
61. Fehrenbach, *Comanches: The History of a People*.
62. See Wikipedia, "Santa Anna (Comanche war chief)," http://en.wikipedia.org/wiki/Santa_Anna_(Comanche_war_chief).
63. See Wikipedia, "Old Owl," http://en.wikipedia.org/wiki/Old_Owl.
64. Ibid.
65. Sloan (or Walnut) Springs was located seven miles southwest of Algerita (31° 09' N, 98° 55' W).
66. Passmore, "Ketemoczy."
67. Texas State Historical Marker #11290.

CHAPTER 4

68. Access Genealogy, "Lipan Apache Indian History," www.accessgenealogy.com/native/tribes/apache/lipan.htm.
69. Dunn, "Apache Relations in Texas," 198–269.

70. Fehrenbach, *Comanches: The Destruction of a People*, 197.
71. See Texas Beyond History, "Pavo Real."
72. Minor, *Turning Adversity to Advantage.*
73. Smith, *From Dominance to Disappearance*, 44 ad passim, 188–189.
74. *San Antonio Ledger*, vol. 2, December 25, 1851.
75. Reeve, "Apache Indians in Texas."
76. Ibid.
77. Thomas F. Schilz, "Castro, Cuelgas De," *Handbook of Texas Online*, www.tshaonline.org/handbook/online/articles/fca92.
78. Moore, *Savage Frontier*, 217.
79. See Lipan Apache Tribe of Texas, "Flacco (abt. 1790–abt. 1850)," www.lipanapache.org/Museum/museum_chiefs.html.
80. Dennis and Dennis, *Life of F.M. Buckelew.*
81. Lehmann, *Nine Years Among the Indians.*
82. Hunter, *Boy Captives.*
83. Berlandier, *Indians of Texas in 1830.*
84. Ruiz, *Report on the Indian Tribes.*
85. Minor, *Turning Adversity to Advantage.*
86. Minor, *Light Gray People*, 54–55.
87. Dennis and Dennis, *Life of F.M. Buckelew.*
88. Ibid.
89. Berlandier, *Indians of Texas in 1830.*
90. Dennis and Dennis, *Life of F.M. Buckelew.*
91. Minor, *Light Gray People*, 57–58.
92. Berlandier, *Indians of Texas in 1830.*
93. Luther, *Camp Verde.*
94. Britten, *Lipan Apaches*, 230.
95. Ibid., 60–61.
96. See Lipan Apache Band of Texas, www.lipanapachebandoftexas.com/index.html.

Chapter 5

97. Bexar County File 129, 1846.
98. Stopka and Black, "Defining the Texas Rangers."
99. Ben H. Procter, "Texas Rangers," *Handbook of Texas Online*, www.tshaonline.org/handbook/online/articles/met04.

100. Herbert Gambrell, "Lamar, Mirabeau Buonaparte," *Handbook of Texas Online*, www.tshaonline.org/handbook/online/articles/fla15.

101. Filibusters, or freebooters, are irregular soldiers who act without authority from their own government and are generally motivated by financial gain, political ideology or the thrill of adventure.

102. De Shields, "Notable Old Texans."

103. Ibid.

104. Lee, *Three Years Among the Comanches.*

105. Gwynne, *Empire of the Summer Moon*, 138.

106. John Coffee "Jack" Hays, Texas Ranger Hall of Fame, www.texasranger.org/halloffame/Hays_John.htm.

107. Enchanted Rock is a spectacular granite pluton in southwestern Llano County about twenty miles north of Fredericksburg, Texas, in the Texas Hill Country. The granite dome rises some 385 feet above the streambed of nearby Sandy Creek to a maximum elevation of 1,825 feet above mean sea level. This great granite monadnock is the second-largest such mountain in the United States (the largest is Stone Mountain, Georgia).

108. Texas Historical Marker #10035; Wilbarger, *Indian Depredations in* Texas.

109. Luther, "Battle of Walker's Creek."

110. Wilbarger, *Indian Depredations in Texas*, 8.

111. Christopher Long, "Wilbarger, John Wesley," *Handbook of Texas Online*, www.tshaonline.org/handbook/online/articles/fwi07.

112. Thomas W. Cutrer, "Walker's Creek, Battle of," *Handbook of Texas Online*, www.tshaonline.org/handbook/online/articles/btw02.

113. See Wikipedia, "Comanche History," http://en.wikipedia.org/wiki/Comanche_history.

114. See Wikipedia, "Texas Ranger Division," http://en.wikipedia.org/wiki/Texas_Ranger_Division.

115. Fehrenbach, *Lone Star*, 276.

116. Wilkins, *Defending the Borders.*

117. See Wikipedia, "Texas Ranger Division," http://en.wikipedia.org/wiki/Texas_Ranger_Division; Ingmire, *Texas Rangers.*

CHAPTER 6

118. Strubberg, *Friedrichsburg.*

119. Morgenthaler, *German Settlement.*

120. Cornelia Marschall Smith and Otto W. Tetzlaff, "Meusebach, John O.," *Handbook of Texas Online*, www.tshaonline.org/handbook/online/articles/fme33.

121. Geue, William and Geue, *New Land Beckoned*; Rippley, *German-Americans*.

122. Smith and Tetzlaff, "Meusebach, John O.," *Handbook*.

123. Rudolph L. Biesele, "Fisher-Miller Land Grant," *Handbook of Texas Online*, www.tshaonline.org/handbook/online/articles/mnf01.

124. King, *John O. Meusebach*.

125. Martin Donell Kohout, "Fredericksburg, Tx," *Handbook of Texas Online*, www.tshaonline.org/handbook/online/articles/hff03.

126. Corker and Humphrey, "Texas Frontier in 1850."

127. Morgenthaler, *German Settlement*, 29.

128. Pedernales River Valley, "History of the Pedernales River Valley."

129. Roemer, *Texas, with Particular Reference*, 232.

130. "Freethinkers" (German *Freidenker*) is a term used to describe some nineteenth-century German intellectuals. Apart from its literal meaning, which suggests an attitude of liberalism unencumbered by dogma and the status quo, the term is also understood to connote agnosticism, if not atheism. However, many of the early freethinkers in Texas were neither true agnostics nor true atheists. Better stated, they considered the notion of deity irrelevant and opposed clerics and churches; if they acknowledged the existence of a traditional Judeo-Christian God, they did not do so with friendliness or affection but as the impatient successors of such belief systems. Lich, *German Texans*.

131. Glen E. Lich, "Bettina, TX," *Handbook of Texas Online*, www.tshaonline.org/handbook/online/articles/hvb55.

132. Pedernales, Texas, was an early settlement of German immigrants in Gillespie County, located seven miles (eleven kilometers) southwest of Fredericksburg, near what is now Texas State Highway 16. The Pedernales school was designated a Recorded Texas Historic Landmark in 1993, Marker #10095.

133. Vivian Elizabeth Smyrl, "Pedernales, Tx," *Handbook of Texas Online*, www.tshaonline.org/handbook/online/articles/hvp27.

134. Biesele, *History of the German Settlements*.

135. See Wikipedia, "Jacob Kuechler," http://en.wikipedia.org/wiki/Jacob_Kuechler.

136. Texas Historic Marker #9444.

137. See Glenn Hadeler, "Kriewitz and the Comanches," Texas Hill Country, www.texfiles.com/hadeler/kriewitz.htm.

138. Biesele, *History of the German Settlements*.

139. Martin Donell Kohout, "Vereins-Kirche," *Handbook of Texas Online*, www.tshaonline.org/handbook/online/articles/ccv01.

140. Biesele, *History of the German Settlements*.

141. Strubberg, *Friedrichsburg: A Novel.*
142. *Fort Martin Scott Newsletter*, "Friedrich Armand Strubberg," Fort Martin Scott, http://fortmartinscott.org/friedrich-armand-strubberg-col.

CHAPTER 7

143. The "Big Empty" is the moniker that Jim W. Corder (1929–1998) called the Texas plains. In his book *Lost in West Texas* (1988), Corder wrote, "The territory I love out there is not much chronicled. In what I have sometimes called the Big Empty, there are, perhaps, only small histories to tell, at least in modern times."
144. Roemer, *Texas, with Particular*, 156.
145. Tilling, *History of the German Element.*
146. Alice J. Rhoades, "Mason, TX," *Handbook of Texas Online*, www.tshaonline.org/handbook/online/articles/hjm06.
147. Vivian Elizabeth Smyrl, "Camp San Saba, Tx," *Handbook of Texas Online*, www.tshaonline.org/handbook/online/articles/hrc13.
148. Bierschwale, "Mason County, Texas."
149. "Katemcy Creek," *Handbook of Texas Online*, www.tshaonline.org/handbook/online/articles/rbk02.
150. Roemer, *Texas, with Particular Reference.*
151. Texas State Historical Marker #4212.
152. See Texas Beyond History, "Los Almagres, the Lost Spanish Mine."
153. Caran, "Lost Spanish Silver Mines," 9–35.
154. Gilmore, "San Luis," *Handbook.*
155. Texas Historical Marker #991.

CHAPTER 8

156. Tilling, *History of the German Element.*
157. Roemer, *Texas, with Particular Reference*, 247.
158. Ibid.
159. Ibid.
160. See Wikipedia, "Emil Kriewitz," http://en.wikipedia.org/wiki/Emil_Kriewitz#Life_with_the_Comanches.
161. Ibid.

Chapter 9

162. Smith, *From Dominance to Disappearance*.
163. Fehrenbach, *Lone Star*, 276.
164. See DailyKos, "Indians 101: The Republic of Texas and the Comanche," www.dailykos.com/story/2010/04/08/855306/-Indians-101-The-Republic-of-Texas-the-Comanche.
165. Smith, *From Dominance to Disappearance*.
166. See Wikipedia, "Robert Neighbors," http://en.wikipedia.org/wiki/Robert_Neighbors.
167. *From Dominance to Disappearance*; Biesele, "Relations between the German Settlers," 116–29.
168. Henry C. Armbruster, "Torrey, John Frink," *Handbook of Texas Online*, www.tshaonline.org/handbook/online/articles/fto22.
169. In 1846, Dr. Ferdinand von Roemer made a trip from New Braunfels to the Brazos post with John Torrey and described the trading house as standing in a post oak grove on a high, pebble-covered hill overlooking Tehuacana Creek. The post comprised six or seven houses built of rough-hewn logs. The largest house held pelts, another contained trade goods for the Indians and the remaining served as living quarters. Henry C. Armbruster, "Torrey Trading Houses," *Handbook of Texas Online*, www.tshaonline.org/handbook/online/articles/dft02.
170. Kappler, *Indian Affairs*.
171. Smith, *From Dominance to Disappearance*, 193.
172. Ibid., 194.
173. Klos, "Indians during Statehood," extract from *Handbook*.
174. Smith, *Frontier Defense*, 4–5.
175. Ibid., 19.
176. Gwynne, *Empire of the Summer Moon*, 162.

Chapter 10

177. Utley, *Frontier Regulars*.
178. Smith, *Old Army in Texas*.
179. Texas State Historical Marker #11277.

Chapter 11

180. Eastman, *Seth Eastman Sketchbook.*
181. National Register Reference #80004121.
182. Texas State Archaeological Landmark 41GL52.
183. Brooks, "Fort Martin Scott," *Handbook*; *Antiquities Code of Texas*, chapter 191, www.thc.state.tx.us/rulesregs/RulesRegsPDF/AntiqCode.pdf.
184. Corker and Humphrey, "Texas Frontier in 1850."
185. Ibid.
186. Lone Star Archeological Services, *First Report on Investigations.*
187. Smith, *U.S. Army and the Texas Frontier Economy*, 34.
188. Crimmins, "W.G. Freeman's Report," 202–8.
189. Wagner and Klein Inc., *Preservation Plan.*
190. Crimmins, "W.G. Freeman's Report."
191. Bexar County Survey No. 36.
192. Gillespie County Deed Records, vol. E, 211.
193. Labadie, *Archaeological Investigation.*
194. *Texas State Times* 2, no. 37 (August 18, 1855), classified ad.

Chapter 12

195. "Wallace Creek (San Saba County)," *Handbook of Texas Online*, www.tshaonline.org/handbook/online/articles/rbw09.
196. Ibid.
197. Recorded Texas Historic Landmark #11290.
198. See Wikipedia, "Fort Martin Scott Treaty," http://en.wikipedia.org/wiki/Fort_Martin_Scott_Treaty.
199. Webb, *Texas Rangers*, 139.

Chapter 13

200. United States Army Center of Military History, "The Artist: Seth Eastman," www.history.army.mil/html/artphoto/pripos/eastman/artist.html.

201. See Wikipedia, "German tradition (*Fachwerkhäuser*)," http://en.wikipedia.org/wiki/Timber_framing#German_tradition_.28Fachwerkh.C3.A4user.29.

202. *Fort Martin Scott Newsletter*, "Seth Eastman," Fort Martin Scott, http://fortmartinscott.org/seth-eastman.

203. United States Army Center of Military History, "The First Regiment of Infantry," compiled in the office of the Military Service Institution, www.history.army.mil/books/R&H/R&H-FM.htm.

204. Luther, *Camp Verde*.

205. Ibid.

CHAPTER 14

206. Luther, "US Army Second Dragoon Regiment."

207. Young, *West of Philip St. George Cooke*.

208. Smith, "U.S. Army Combat Operations," 501–31.

209. Second Cavalry Association Regimental History Center, http://history.dragoons.org.

210. Margaret Bierschwale, "Hamilton Wilcox Merrill," *Handbook of Texas Online*, www.tshaonline.org/handbook/online/articles/fme28.

211. United States Army, Returns from Regular Army Cavalry Regiments, 1833–1916, microfilm no. M744, Rolls 14–16.

212. Cooke, *Scenes and Adventures*.

213. Julius E. DeVos. "Fort Mason," *Handbook of Texas Online*, www.tshaonline.org/handbook/online/articles/qbf34.

CHAPTER 15

214. Wilhelm, *History of the Eighth U.S. Infantry*.

215. Ibid.

216. H.E. Haass, "Fort Lincoln," *Handbook of Texas Online*, www.tshaonline.org/handbook/online/articles/qbf31.

217. Nardo and Nofi, *James Longstreet*, 58–59.

218. See Wikipedia, "James Longstreet," http://en.wikipedia.org/wiki/James_Longstreet#Early_life_and_career.

219. Dodge, *Our Wild Indians.*

220. Kime, *Colonel Richard Irving Dodge.*

221. Dodge, *Our Wild Indians.*

222. Ibid., 92.

223. Thomas W. Cutrer and David Paul Smith, "Twiggs, David Emanuel," *Handbook of Texas Online*, www.tshaonline.org/handbook/online/articles/ftw03.

224. Thompson, *Texas and New Mexico*, 183.

225. Luther, *Camp Verde*, 127.

CHAPTER 16

226. Price, *Across the Continent.*

227. Arnold, *Jeff Davis's Own.*

228. Fehrenbach, *Comanches: The Destruction of a People*, 424–25.

229. Ibid., 32–36.

230. Price, *Across the Continent*, 31

231. Arnold, *Jeff Davis's Own*, 32–36.

232. See Wikipedia, "Little Ice Age," http://en.wikipedia.org/wiki/Little_Ice_Age.

233. Price, *Across the Continent*, 35.

234. Recorded Texas Historic Landmark #11275.

235. United States Army, Returns from Regular Army Cavalry Regiments, microfilm no. M744, Second Cavalry, 1849–55, Roll 16.

CHAPTER 17

236. See Wikipedia, "Texas in the American Civil War," http://en.wikipedia.org/wiki/Texas_in_the_American_Civil_War.

237. Norment and Kibler, *Archeological Survey of the Proposed Site.*

238. Ralph A. Wooster, "Civil War," *Handbook of Texas Online*, www.tshaonline.org/handbook/online/articles/qdc02.

239. Walter L. Buenger, "Unionism," *Handbook of Texas Online*, www.tshaonline.org/handbook/online/articles/mzu01.

240. Texas State Historical Association, "Texas Germans Declare Slavery to Be Evil," www.tshaonline.org/day-by-day/30705.

241. Texas State Archives and Library Commission, "Dissent: Under the Rebel Flag," https://www.tsl.state.tx.us/exhibits/civilwar/dissent.html.

242. Luther, "Civil War Trails in Kerr County."

243. University of Texas Libraries, "An Inventory of Adjutant General's Texas State Troops Records at the Texas State Archives, 1861–1865, undated," www.lib.utexas.edu/taro/tslac/30174/tsl-30174.html.

244. Robert W. Shook, "James Duff," *Handbook of Texas Online*, www.tshaonline.org/handbook/online/articles/fdu06.

245. Luther, *Camp Verde*, 120; Hoffman, "Blackest Crime in Texas Warfare."; Shook. "Duff, James," *Handbook*.

246. Schulz, "Nueces Massacre."

247. Luther, *Camp Verde*, 120.

248. William Banta—Indian fighter, Civil War soldier and autobiographer—organized and commanded the first company of minutemen in Burnet County and participated in nearly every engagement against Indians in the region throughout the 1850s. He saw service on the Texas frontier during the Civil War as lieutenant, then captain, of Company A of the Frontier Regiment. With J.W. Caldwell, he wrote an account of his life in Texas, *Twenty-Seven Years on the Texas Frontier*, published in 1893.

249. Baluch, *Dogs of War Unleashed.*

250. Ransleben, *Hundred Years of Comfort.*

251. Mark Lye, "Tegener, Frederick [Fritz]," *Handbook of Texas Online*, www.tshaonline.org/handbook/online/articles/fte55.

252. Schwethelm, "I Was a Survivor."

253. Baluch, *Dogs of War Unleashed.*

254. Van Winkle, "Myth, Fate Clash," 1.

255. Williams and Sansom, *Massacre on the Nueces River*; Schulz, "Nueces Massacre."

256. Luther, *Camp Verde.*

257. Underwood, *Death on the Nueces.*

258. "Nueces, Battle of the," *Handbook of Texas Online*, www.tshaonline.org/handbook/online/articles/qfn01.

259. Williams and Sansom, *Massacre on the Nueces River.*

260. Schwethelm, "I Was a Survivor"; Williams and Sansom, *Massacre on the Nueces River.*

261. Henry Schwethelm, a survivor of the Unionist group massacred at the Nueces River, Texas, in August 1862, left an account of events in 1923 that originally appeared in the *San Antonio Express* newspaper in August 1924, and also in the *Bandera Frontier Times*, vol. 2, no. 1 (October 1924).

262. Texas Historical Marker #15.

263. National Register Listing #78002966.

264. "Nueces, Battle of the," *Handbook.*

265. Banta and Cadwell, *Narrative, 1893.*

266. David Paul Smith, "Banta, William," *Handbook of Texas Online*, www.tshaonline.org/handbook/online/articles/fba58.

267. Banta and Cadwell, *Twenty-Seven Years.*

268. Norment and Kibler, *Archeological Survey of the Proposed Site*, 8.

269. Texas State Historical Marker #10050.

270. University of Texas Libraries, "Adjutant General's Texas State Troops Records at the Texas State Archives: Camp Davis," www.lib.utexas.edu/taro/tslac/30174/tsl-30174.html.

271. "Jayhawker" is here defined as a Unionist guerilla.

272. Robert Dunnam, "Frontier Regiment," *Handbook of Texas Online*, www.tshaonline.org/handbook/online/articles/qjf01.

273. Luther, *Camp Verde.*

274. Carter, *Rebel Outlaw.*

275. Ramsdell, "Texas from the Fall of the Confederacy."

276. Fehrenbach, *Comanches: The Destruction of a People*, 494.

Chapter 18

277. Crimmins, "Fourth Cavalry in Texas."

278. *Texas State Times*, vol. 2, no. 37 (August 18, 1855).

279 Hutton, *Phil Sheridan and His Army*, 180.

280. Ramsdell, "Texas from the Fall of the Confederacy."

281. Luther, "Shootout at Schreiner's."

282. See Wikipedia, "Fifth Military District," http://en.wikipedia.org/wiki/Fifth_Military_District.

283. Keliher, *History of the Fourth U.S. Cavalry.*

284. Wallace, *Ranald S. Mackenzie.*

285. The 1950 John Ford movie *Rio Grande* has some similarities to his action on the frontier. The 1958–59 syndicated television series *Mackenzie's Raiders*, starring Richard Carlson in the title role, is loosely based on Mackenzie's time in Texas.

CHAPTER 19

286. Braeutigam Family History, http://braeutigamfamilyhistory.homestead.com/JW_Braeutigam_chapter.pdf.
287. Gillespie County Fair & Festivals Association History website.
288. Van Winkle, "Braeutigam-Kensing Tales Rife."
289. Fort Martin Scott brochure, Fredericksburg, Texas.
290. Van Winkle, "Braeutigam-Kensing Tales Rife."

CHAPTER 20

291. Smith, *From Dominance to Disappearance*, 205.
292. Camp Johnson is on the North Concho River, fifteen miles northwest of present-day San Angelo.
293. Smith, *From Dominance to Disappearance*, 205–6.
294. Ibid., 211.
295. Carrie J. Crouch, "Brazos Indian Reservation," *Handbook of Texas Online*, www.tshaonline.org/handbook/online/articles/bpb03.
296. W.E.S. Dickerson, "Comanche Indian Reservation," *Handbook of Texas Online*, www.tshaonline.org/handbook/online/articles/bpc10.
297. See a page from the *Texas Almanac for 1859*, "The Indian Reserves of Texas," Portal to Texas History, http://texashistory.unt.edu/ark:/67531/metapth123765.
298. Charles G. Davis, "Camp Cooper," *Handbook of Texas Online*, www.tshaonline.org/handbook/online/articles/qbc09.
299. Kenmotsu and Wade, "Ethnohistory"; U.S. Bureau of Indian Affairs.
300. Ibid.
301. Klos, "Indians during Statehood," extract from *Handbook*.
302. Jerry Thompson, "Baylor, John Robert." *Texas Handbook Online*, www.tshaonline.org/handbook/online/articles/fbaat.
303. Texas History, "Texas' Indian Reservations." http://texashistory.com/Archives/TexasIndianReservations/tabid/152/language/en-US/Default.aspx.
304. H. Allen Anderson, "Goodnight, Charles," *Handbook of Texas Online*, www.tshaonline.org/handbook/online/articles/fgo11.
305. See Wikipedia, "Fort Sill," http://en.wikipedia.org/wiki/Fort_Sill.
306. Wallace, *Ranald S. Mackenzie*.

307. Neighbours, *Robert Simpson Neighbors*.
308. William Burnet to David Burnett, letter, October 29, 1859, and J.M. Smith report in Seguin, Texas *Union Democrat*, October 8, 1859, http://texashistory.com/Archives/TexasIndianReservations/tabid/152/language/en-US/Default.asp.

Appendix

309. Prewitt, *National Register of Historic Places Nomination Form—Fort Martin Scott*.
310. Center for Archaeological Research—Department of Anthropology/College of Liberal and Fine Arts, University of Texas–San Antonio, www.car.utsa.edu.
311. Labadie, *Archeological Investigations*.
312. Kegley and Black, "Archeological Testing at Fort Martin Scott."
313. Labadie, *Archeological Investigations*.
314. This entire analysis is from Labadie, *Archeological Investigations*.
315. A sutler, or victualer, is a civilian merchant who sells provisions to an army in the field, in camp or in quarters. See Wikipedia, "Sutler." http://en.wikipedia.org/wiki/Sutler.
316. Corker and Humphrey, "Texas Frontier in 1850."

Archaeological References for Fort Martin Scott

Blake, Marie E., and Martha Doty Freeman. *Archeological Survey of the Proposed Texas Tech University Campus, Gillespie County, Texas*. Letter Report No. 486. Austin, TX: Prewitt and Associates Inc., 2001.

Fox, Anne A. *Monitoring of Electrical Installation at Fort Martin Scot, Gillespie County, Texas.* TAC Permit 688. Fredericksburg, TX: Wagner and Klein Architects, 1988. Letter report submitted to Texas Antiquities Committee.

Jernigan, R.E. "Fort Martin Scott Update: The 1992 Field Season Begins." *Field Notes* 5, no. 1 (1992). Newsletter of the Travis County Archeological Society.

Kegley, George, and Arthur Black. "Archeological Testing at Fort Martin Scott, 1991–1993, Buildings B, C and P." Unpublished manuscript for Archaeological Resource Evaluation Associates, Austin, Texas, 1994.

Labadie, Joseph H. *Archaeological Investigation at Fort Martin Scott (41GL52) in Gillespie County, Texas*. Center for Archaeological Research at the University of Texas–San Antonio, Archaeological Survey Report, No. 169, 1987.

Lone Star Archaeological Services. *First Report on Investigations at Fort Martin Scott, U.S.A. (1848–1853), Near Fredericksburg, Gillespie County, Texas: The Search for Building A & R*. Fredericksburg, TX: Fredericksburg Heritage Foundation, 1996.

Norment, Aaron, and Karl W. Kibler. *Archeological Survey of the Proposed Site of the Former Texas Rangers Museum, City of Fredericksburg, Gillespie County, Texas*. Ross C. Fields, Principal Investigator. Austin, TX: Prewitt and Associates, 2012.

Parschall and Associates Architects. *Site Plan for Barracks Building B at Fort Martin Scott.* Austin, TX: self-published, 1999.

Ringstaff, Christopher W., and Jennifer K. Williams. *Phase 2 Investigations of the Proposed Texas Tech Campus, Gillespie County, Texas.* Technical Report, No. 53. Austin, TX: Prewitt and Associates, 2002.

Saner, Bryant, Jr. "Magnetometer Survey of a Portion of Fort Martin Scott (41GL52), Gillespie County, Texas." Unpublished manuscript for the Hill Country Archaeological Association, Kerrville, Texas, 2002.

———. "Shovel Testing at Fort Martin Scott, 41GL52, Gillespie County, Texas." *Ancient Echoes* (2003). Journal of the Hill Country Archeological Association, Kerrville, Texas.

Tomka, Marybeth. "Work at Fort Martin Scott Begins for TCAS." *Field Notes* 4, no. 2 (1991). Newsletter of the Travis County Archeological Society.

Wagner and Klein Inc. *Preservation Plan for Fort Martin Scott, Fredericksburg, Texas.* Fredericksburg, TX: Fredericksburg Heritage Foundation, 1983.

Wright, K. *Excavation of Officer's Quarters "C" at Fort Martin Scott (41GL52), Fredericksburg, Texas.* Report submitted to Texas Antiquities Committee on satisfaction of Permit No. 12011993.

Select Bibliography

Arnold, James R. *Jeff Davis's Own: Cavalry, Comanches, and the Battle for the Texas Frontier.* New York: Wiley, 2000.

Baluch, Joe. *The Dogs of War Unleashed: The Devil Concealed in Men Unchained.* Lubbock: West Texas Historical Association, 1997.

Banta, William, and John Wesley Cadwell Jr. *Narrative, 1893.* Austin: Dolph Briscoe Center for American History, University of Texas at Austin.

———. *Twenty-Seven Years on the Frontier, or Fifty Years in Texas.* N.p.: B.C. Jones & Company, 1893.

Berlandier, Juan-Luis. *Indians of Texas in 1830.* Edited by John C. Ewers and translated by Patricia Reading Leclerq. Washington, D.C.: Smithsonian, 1969.

Betty, Gerald. *Comanche Society: Before the Reservation.* College Station: Texas A&M University Press, 2005.

Bexar County Survey No. 36, December 4, 1845. Bexar County, Texas.

Bierschwale, Margaret. "Mason County, Texas, 1845–1870." *Southwestern Historical Quarterly* 52 (April 1949).

Biesele, R.I. "The Relations Between the German Settlers and the Indians in Texas, 1844–1860." *Southwestern Historical Quarterly* 31, no. 2 (October 1927): 116–29.

Biesele, Rudolph L. *The History of the German Settlements in Texas, 1831–1861.* Austin, TX: Von Boeckmann-Jones, 1930.

Boeck, Brian J. "They Contributed Very Much to the Success of Our Colony." *Southwestern Historical Quarterly* 105 (July 2001–April 2002).

Brice, Donaly E. *The Great Comanche Raid: Boldest Indian Attack on the Texas Republic.* Weldon, NC: McGowan Book Company, 1987.

Britten, Thomas A. *The Lipan Apaches: People of Wind and Lightning*. Albuquerque: University of New Mexico Press, 2009.

Burnet, David G. "The Comanches and Other Tribes of Texas; and the Policy to be Pursued Respecting Them." *Historical and Statistical Information Respecting the History, Conditions, and Prospects of the Indian Tribes of the United States.* 9 vols. Edited by Henry R. Schoolcraft. Philadelphia: Lippincott, Grambo, 1851.

Caldwell, Clifford R. *A Day's Ride from Here*. Vol 2. *Noxville, Texas.* Charleston, SC: The History Press, 2011.

Campbell, Randolph B. *Gone to Texas*. New York: Oxford University Press, 2004.

Caran, S. Christopher. "The Lost Spanish Silver Mines of Llano County, Texas." *Texas Heritage* 18, no. 4 (2000): 9–35.

Carter, Forrest. *The Rebel Outlaw: Josey Wales.* Albuquerque: University of New Mexico Press, 1989.

Catlin, George. *North American Indians*. Edited by Peter Matthiessen. New York: Penguin Books, 1989.

Center for Archaeological Research—Department of Anthropology/College of Liberal and Fine Arts, University of Texas–San Antonio. www.car.utsa.edu.

Chipman, Donald E., and Robert S. Weddle. "How Historical Myths Are Born…and Why They Seldom Die." *Southwestern Historical Quarterly* 116, no. 1 (January 2013).

Cooke, Philip St. George. *Scenes and Adventures in the Army or Romances of Military Life.* Philadelphia: Lindsay & Blakiston, 1859.

Corker, Caleb, and Janet G. Humphrey. "The Texas Frontier in 1850: Dr. Ebenezer Swift and the View from Fort Martin Scott." *Southwestern Historical Quarterly* 96 (July 1992–April 1993).

Cox, Mike. *The Texas Rangers*. Vol. 1, *Wearing the Cinco Peso 1821–1900*. New York: Tom Doherty Associates, 2008.

Crimmins, M.L. "The Fourth Cavalry in Texas." *Frontier Times* 15, no. 5 (February 1938).

———. "W.G. Freeman's Report on the Eighth Military Department." *Southwestern Historical Quarterly* 53, no.1 (1949): 202–8.

Dennis, T.S., and Mrs. T.S. Dennis. *The Life of F.M. Buckelew, the Indian Captive as Related by Himself.* Kerrville, TX: Herring Publishing, 1925.

De Shields, James T. "Notable Old Texans of the Pioneer Era: John H. Moore." *Dallas Morning News Magazine*, August 11, 1907.

Dixon, Olive. *Life of Billy Dixon*. Dallas, TX: Southwest Press, 1914.

Dodge, Richard Irving. *Our Wild Indians: Thirty-Three Years' Personal Experience Among the Red Men of the Great West*. Hartford, CT: A.D. Worthington and Company, 2008.

Dunn, William E. "Apache Relations in Texas, 1718–1750." *Texas State Historical Association Quarterly* 14, no. 3 (January 1911).

Eastman, Seth. *A Seth Eastman Sketchbook, 1848–1849*. Introduction by Lois Burkhalter. Austin: University of Texas Press, 2003.

Edwards, Walter. *The Story of Fredericksburg*. Fredericksburg, TX: Fredericksburg Chamber of Commerce, 1969.

———. *Tales of Old Fredericksburg*. Morgantown, WV: Gargoyle Press, 1974.

Fehrenbach, T.R. *Comanches: The Destruction of a People*. Cambridge, MA: De Capo Press, 1974.

———. *Comanches: The History of a People*. New York: Anchor, 2003.

———. *Lone Star: A History of Texas and the Texans*. Cambridge, MA: Da Capo Press, 2000.

Ford, John Salmon. *Rip Ford's Texas*. Austin: University of Texas Press, 1987.

Fort Martin Scott. http://fortmartinscott.org.

Geue, Mayo, Chester William and Ethel H. Geue. *A New Land Beckoned: German Immigration to Texas, 1844–1847*. Waco, TX: Texian Press, 1966.

Gillespie County Deed Records. Vol. E, 211. Gillespie County, Texas.

Gillespie County Fair & Festivals Association History. www.gillespiefair.com/about-gillespie-county-fair-festivals-association.htm.

Gillespie County Historical Society. "Pioneers in God's Hills." Fredericksburg, TX: Fredericksburg Publishing, 1925.

Greer, James K. *Texas Ranger: Jack Hays in the Frontier Southwest*. College Station: Texas A&M University Press, 1993.

Gwynne, S.C. *Empire of the Summer Moon: Quanah Parker and the Rise and Fall of the Comanches, the Most Powerful Indian Tribe in American History*. New York: Scribner, 2010.

Hämäläinen, Pekka. *The Comanche Empire*. New Haven, CT: Yale University Press, 2009.

Hester, Thomas R. "Early Human Populations Along the Balcones Escarpment." *The Balcones Escarpment, Central Texas*. Edited by Patrick L. Abbott and C.M. Woodruff Jr. www.lib.utexas.edu/geo/balcones_escarpment/contents.html.

Hoffman, A. "The Blackest Crime in Texas Warfare." *Dallas Morning News*, May 5, 1929.

Hunter, J. Marvin. *The Boy Captives: Being the True Story of the Experiences and Hardships of Clinton L. Smith and Jeff D. Smith*. San Sabá, TX: San Saba Printing, 2002.

Hutton, Paul Andrew. *Phil Sheridan and His Army*. Norman: University of Oklahoma Press, 1999.

Ingmire, Frances T. *Texas Rangers: Frontier Battalion, Minute Men, Commanding Officers, 1847–1900*. St. Louis, MO: Ingmire Publications, 1982.

Ivey, Darren L. *The Texas Rangers: A Registry and History*. Jefferson, NC: McFarland & Company, 2010.

Jenkins, John Holmes, III, ed. *Recollections of Early Texas: Memoirs of John Holland Jenkins*. Austin: University of Texas Press, 1987.

Kappler, Charles J., comp. and ed. *Indian Affairs: Laws and Treaties*. Vol. 2, *Treaties*. Washington, D.C.: Government Printing Office, 1904. http://digital.library.okstate.edu/kappler/vol2/treaties/com0554.htm.

Keliher, John G. *The History of the Fourth U.S. Cavalry Regiment*. http://cav_trooper0.tripod.com/cavalrycountryusa/id115.html.

Kenmotsu, Nancy A., and Mariah F. Wade. "Ethnohistory, 1750–1880." Chap. 3 in *American Indian Tribal Affiliation Study*. Phase 1, *Ethnohistoric Literature Review*. Del Rio: published jointly by Texas Department of Transportation, Environmental Affairs Division and National Park Service, Amistad National Recreation Area, 2002. www.nps.gov/history/history/online_books/amis/aspr-34/chap3.htm.

Kime, Wayne R. *Colonel Richard Irving Dodge: The Life and Times of a Career Army Officer*. Norman: University of Oklahoma Press, 2006.

King, Irene Marschall. *John O. Meusebach: German Organizer in Texas*. Austin: University of Texas Press, 1967.

Knopp, Ken. *German Immigration to America: The Fredericksburg Texas Manuscripts*. Fredericksburg, TX: self published, 1999.

Koch, Lena Clara. "The Federal Indian Policy in Texas, 1846–1860." *Southwest Historical Quarterly* 29, no. 24 (1925).

Lee, Nelson. *Three Years Among the Comanches*. Albany NY: Baker Taylor Company, 1859.

Lehmann, Herman. *Nine Years Among the Indians 1870–1879*. Edited by J. Marvin Hunter. Austin, TX: Von Beockmann-Jones Company, 1927.

Lich, Glen E. *The German Texans*. San Antonio: University of Texas Institute of Texan Cultures, 1981.

Lipan Apache Tribe of Texas. www.lipanapache.org.

Luther, Joseph. "Battle of Walker's Creek: Jack Hays and the Paterson Colt Five-Shot Revolving Pistol." *Kerrville Daily Times*, 2010.

———. *Camp Verde: Texas Frontier Defense*. Charleston, SC: The History Press, 2012.

———. "Civil War Trails in Kerr County, Texas." Kerrville, Texas. Kerr County Chamber of Commerce. http://kerrvilletx.wordpress.com/2009/11/06/civil-war-trails-in-kerr-county-tx.

———. "The Penetaka Comanche." *Kerrville Daily Times*, 2010.

———. "Shootout at Schreiner's: 1873 Gunfight in Downtown Kerrville." *Kerrville Daily Times*, n.d.

———. "US Army Second Dragoon Regiment in Kerr County." *Kerrville Daily Times*, 2010.

McGowen, Stanley S. *Horse Sweat and Powder Smoke: The First Texas Cavalry in the Civil War*. College Station: Texas A&M University Press, 1999.

Minor, Nancy McGowen. *The Light Gray People: An Ethno-History of the Lipan Apaches of Texas and Northern Mexico*. Lanham, MD: University Press of America, 2009.

———. *Turning Adversity to Advantage: A History of the Lipan Apaches of Texas and Northern Mexico, 1700–1900*. Lanham, MD: University Press of America, 2009.

Moore, Stephen L. *Savage Frontier*. Vol. 4, *1842–1845: Rangers, Riflemen and Indian Wars in Texas*. Denton: University of North Texas Press, 2010.

Morgenthaler, Jefferson. *The German Settlement of the Texas Hill Country*. Seattle, WA: Mockingbird Books, 2007.

Nardo, R.L., and Albert A. Nofi. *James Longstreet: The Man, the Soldier, the Controversy*. New York: Da Capo Press, 1998.

Neighbours, Kenneth Franklin. *Robert Simpson Neighbors and the Texas Frontier, 1836–1859*. Waco: Texian Press, 1975.

Newcomb, W.W., Jr. *The Indians of Texas: From Prehistoric to Modern Times*. Austin: University of Texas Press, 1961.

Passmore, Leonard. "Ketemoczy." *Frontier Times* 4, no. 2 (1926).

Pedernales River Valley. "The History of the Pedernales River Valley." www.pedernalesrivervalley.com/texashillcountryhistory.htm.

Penniger, Robert. *Festival Edition for the Fifteenth Anniversary Jubilee of the Founding of the City of Fredericksburg*. Fredericksburg, TX: Fredericksburg Publishing, 1971.

Portal to Texas History. http://texashistory.unt.edu.

Prewitt, E.R. "National Register of Historic Places Nomination Form—Fort Martin Scott," May 2, 1979. National Park Service, Washington, D.C. http://www.nps.gov/nr.

Price, George F. *Across the Continent with the Fifth Cavalry*. New York: Van Nostrand, 1883.

Rampp, Larry C. "William C. Quantrill's Civil War Activities in Texas, 1861–1863." *Texas Military History* 8 (1970).

Ramsdell, Charles W. "Texas from the Fall of the Confederacy to the Beginning of Reconstruction." *Quarterly of the Texas State Historical Association* 11 (January 1908).

Ransleben, Guido. *A Hundred Years of Comfort in Texas*. San Antonio, TX: Naylor, 1954.

Reeve, Frank D. "The Apache Indians in Texas." *Southwestern Historical Quarterly* 50 (October 1946).

Richardson, Rupert N. *The Comanche Barrier to South Plains Settlement: A Century and a Half of Savage Resistance to the Advancing White Frontier*. Glendale, CA: Arthur H. Clarke Company, 1933.

Richter, William L. *The Army in Texas during Reconstruction, 1865–1870*. College Station: Texas A&M University Press, 1987.

Rippley, La Vern. *The German-Americans*. Boston: Twayne Publishers, 1976.

Roemer, Ferdinand. *Texas, with Particular Reference to German Immigration and the Physical Appearance of the Country*. Translated by Oswald Mueller. San Antonio, TX: Standard, 1935. Reprint, Waco, TX: Texian, 1967.

Ruiz, Jose Francisco. *Report on the Indian Tribes of Texas in 1828*. Facsimile and translation edited with an introduction by John C. Ewers and translated by Georgette Dorn. New Haven, CT: Yale University Press, 1972.

Schulz, Robert G., Jr. "The Nueces Massacre, Also Known as the Battle of the Nueces." Shon Powers' Civil War Blog. http://fspowerscw.blogspot.com/2006/08/nueces-massacre-also-known-as-battle.html.

Schwethelm, H.J. "I Was a Survivor of the Nueces Battle." As told to Albert Schutze. *San Antonio Press*. "Frontier Times Section," August 31, 1924.

Simpson, Harold B. *Cry Comanche: The Second U.S. Cavalry in Texas*. Hillsboro, TX: Hill Junior College Press, 1979.

Smith, David Paul. *Frontier Defense in the Civil War: Texas Rangers and Rebels*. College Station: Texas A&M University Press, 2009.

Smith, F. Todd. *From Dominance to Disappearance: The Indians of Texas and the Near Southwest, 1786–1859*. Lincoln: University of Nebraska Press, 2005.

Smith, Thomas T. *The Old Army in Texas: A Research Guide to the U.S. Army in Nineteenth-Century Texas*. Austin: Austin, Texas State Historical Association, 2000.

———. *The U.S. Army and the Texas Frontier Economy, 1845–1900*. Austin: University of Texas Press, 1999.

———. "U.S. Army Combat Operations in the Indian Wars of Texas, 1849–1881." *Southwestern Historical Quarterly* 99, no. 4 (1996).

Stopka, Christina, and Tony Black. "Defining the Texas Rangers." Official Texas Ranger Hall of Fame and Museum. www.texasranger.org/ReCenter/captains.pdf.

Strubberg, Friedrich Armand. *Friedrichsburg: A Novel*. Translated, annotated and illustrated by James C. Kearney. Austin: University of Texas Press, 2012.

———. *Friedrichsburg: Colony of the German Furstenverein*. Translated by James C. Kearney. Austin: University of Texas Press, 2012.

The Texas Almanac for 1859. "The Indian Reserves of Texas." University of North Texas Libraries, Portal to Texas History, Texas State Historical Association, Denton, Texas. http://texashistory.unt.edu/ark:/67531/metapth123765.

Texas Beyond History. www.texasbeyondhistory.net.

Texas Hill Country. www.texfiles.com.

Texas History. http://texashistory.com.

Texas Ranger Hall of Fame. www.texasranger.org.

Texas State Archives and Library Commission. https://www.tsl.state.tx.us.

Texas State Historical Association. *Handbook of Texas Online*. Various articles. www.tshaonline.org/handbook/online.

Thompson, Jerry. *Texas and New Mexico on the Eve of the Civil War*. Albuquerque: University of New Mexico Press, 2001.

Tilling, Moritz. *History of the German Element in Texas from 1820–1850.* Houston, TX: M. Tilling, 1913.

Underwood, Rodman L. *Death on the Nueces: German Texans, Treue der Union.* Austin, TX: Eakin Press, 2000.

United States Army. Returns from Regular Army Cavalry Regiments, 1833–1916. Microfilm no. M744. Rolls 14–16. National Archives and Records Administration, Washington, D.C.

———. Returns from Regular Army Cavalry Regiments, Second Cavalry, 1849–1855. Microfilm no. M744. Roll 16. National Archives and Records Administration, Washington, D.C.

United States Army Center of Military History. www.history.army.mil.

Utley, Robert M. *Frontier Regulars the United States Army and the Indian, 1866–1891.* Lincoln: University of Nebraska Press, 1971.

Van Winkle, Irene. "Braeutigam-Kensing Tales Rife with Woe." *West Kerr Current.* http://wkcurrent.com/braeutigamkensing-tales-rife-with-woe-p1849-71.htm.

———. "Myth, Fate Clash Around Tegener's Role in Unionist Movement." *West Kerr Current,* October 1, 2008.

Wade, Maria F., and Don E. Wade. *The Native Americans of the Texas Edwards Plateau, 1582–1799.* Austin: University of Texas Press, 2002.

Wallace, Ernest. *Ranald S. Mackenzie on the Texas Frontier.* Lubbock: West Texas Museum Association, 1964.

———. *Texas in Turmoil.* Austin, TX: Steck-Vaughn Company, 1965.

Webb, Walter Prescott. *The Texas Rangers.* Boston: Houghton Mifflin, 1935. Reprint, Austin: University of Texas Press, 1982.

Wilbarger, J.W. *Indian Depredations in* Texas. Austin, TX: Hutchings Printing House, 1889. Reprint, Austin, TX: Eakin Press, 1985.

Wilhelm, Thomas. *History of the Eighth U.S. Infantry, From Its Organization in 1838.* 2 vols. New York: Headquarters, Eighth Infantry, 1873.

Wilkins, Frederick. *Defending the Borders: The Texas Rangers, 1848–1861.* Buffalo Gap, TX: State House Press, 2001.

Williams, J.W. *Old Texas Trails.* Edited by Kenneth F. Neighbors. Burnet, TX: Eakin Press, 1979.

Williams, R.H. *With the Border Ruffians: Memories of the Far West, 1852–1868.* Lincoln, NE: Bison Press, 1982.

Williams, R.H., and John W. Sansom. *Massacre on the Nueces River: Story of a Civil War Tragedy.* Found at University of North Texas Libraries, Portal to Texas History. http://texashistory.unt.edu/ark:/67531/metapth2409.

Wilson, Richard H., Adjutant, Eighth U.S. Infantry. *The Eighth Regiment of Infantry.* N.p., n.d. http://www.history.army.mil/books/R&H/R&H-8IN.htm.

Young, Otis E. *The West of Philip St. George Cooke, 1809–1895*. Glendale, CA: Arthur H. Clark Company, 1955.

INDEX

About the Author

Joseph Luther is a sixth-generation Texan who lives in Kerrville, Texas. He earned his doctorate at Texas A&M University and is a Professor Emeritus of the University of Nebraska–Lincoln, where he taught for twenty-three years, serving as associate dean of the College of Architecture. He also taught for ten years at Eastern Washington University. An enthusiastic avocational archaeologist and historian, Dr. Luther is a member in the Hill Country Archaeological Association and is its webmaster (www.hcarcheology.org). He is also an active member of the Texas State Historical Association, Texas Archaeological Society, South Texas Archaeological Association and the Historical Archaeology Association. Dr. Luther is a correspondent for the *Kerrville Daily Times* and has written a number of articles about Texas history. He was recently named Archaeologist of the Year for 2012 by the Hill Country Archaeological Association. His last book, *Camp Verde: Texas Frontier Defense* (The History Press) was a bestseller in 2012.

THEN & NOW®

VACAVILLE

Carole Noske and Brian Irwin
Vacaville Heritage Council

This book is dedicated to the memory of Bertram "Bert" Hughes, the founders, and the members of the Vacaville Heritage Council who had the foresight to preserve Old Town Hall as a repository of the memories of Vacaville and Solano County.

ISBN 978-0-7385-5563-8

Library of Congress control number: 2007928548

Published by Arcadia Publishing
Charleston, South Carolina

Printed in the United States of America

Then and Now is a registered trademark and is used under license from Salamander Books Limited

For all general information contact Arcadia Publishing at:
Telephone 843-853-2070
Fax 843-853-0044
E-mail sales@arcadiapublishing.com
For customer service and orders:
Toll-Free 1-888-313-2665

Visit us on the Internet at www.arcadiapublishing.com

On the Front Cover: The buildings on the east side of the 600 block of Main Street are some of the oldest commercial buildings remaining in Vacaville. With the exception of the 1920 bank building on the corner, all were constructed using brick shortly after fire destroyed the entire business district in 1884. On April 19, 1892, an earthquake toppled the facades of many buildings along Main Street, but they were quickly repaired, and these buildings remain completely occupied to this day. (Courtesy Vacaville Heritage Council.)

On the Back Cover: Always looking for a reason to have a parade, two were held on July 4, 1898. This one, with the theme "Remember the Maine!", followed by a children's parade for the dedication of the new high school. The Masonic Hall shown on the left was destroyed by fire in May 1939, and newer buildings have replaced most of the other structures on the west side of the street. (Courtesy Vacaville Heritage Council.)

Contents

ACKNOWLEDGMENTS

A special thank you belongs to all the families of Vacaville and Solano County who over the years have shared their photographs, memories, and memorabilia with the Vacaville Heritage Council. All images in this book are courtesy of the Vacaville Heritage Council and the authors.

Thank you also to our historians past and present: Bert Hughes, Bob Allen, Jerry Bowen, Thomas Buckingham, Art Dietz, Dave Fleming, Wiley Killingsworth, John and Richard Rico, Rodney Rulofson, Sabine Goerke-Shrode, Ernest Wichels, Wood Young, and many others for their writings, research, photography, and guidance.

For their photographic work in the late 1800s, which is treasured by all, we can not fail to recognize Prof. Otto Ryhiner with his pinhole camera, whose images were damaged by fire, and Edlif Pyle for rescuing them and adding his own views of Vacaville and the Valleys.

The hands of many volunteers at the Vacaville Heritage Council have contributed to compiling and archiving the memories shown on these pages, foremost among them Ruth Holtz, who kept everything in order, and Roberta (Gates) Ormas, who established and cataloged our history library dedicated in her name. We regret that space does not allow acknowledging every one of our volunteers by name.

And lastly thanks to Jerry Bowen, who convinced us to do this book and has provided support throughout the project.

Introduction

Vacaville is situated at the point where the south end of Vaca Valley opens into the Central Valley of California at an elevation of 180 feet. The sharp contours of the English Hills separate the Vaca Valley from the Central Valley on the east. Beyond a low range of hills to the west is Lagoon Valley. Farther west, the Vaca Mountains rise to an elevation of 2,000 feet four miles from the city.

The lush valley was first home to a Native American population of Patwin Indians known as the "Ulatis" who occupied an area that included the Lagoon Valley and the very heart of town. In 1842, Spanish settlers Manual Vaca and Juan Felipe Peña came from New Mexico and applied for a Mexican land grant. They each built an adobe dwelling on adjoining parcels in Lagoon Valley; the Peña Adobe survives to this day as a state historic landmark.

On August 21, 1850, Manual Vaca sold a square English league of land to William McDaniel with the provision that one square mile was developed as a town to be named Vacaville. Incorporated in 1892, the economy was based almost entirely on cattle and fruit cultivation until the post–World War II era. The climate gave Vacaville an advantage in the marketplace, and it became known as the "early fruit district." Fruit shipments to the eastern market was the source of many a family's fortune, and this is reflected in structures that were erected during that time period, many of which remain to this day.

During the early years, the town suffered several devastating fires—one in 1877 and another on the night of November 7, 1888. Driven by a north wind, within minutes it consumed all the buildings on the north side of Main Street all the way to the bridge, and jumping across Main, the fire claimed the Davis Hotel and the others structures back to Elizabeth Street. Even after the destructive 1877 fire, Vacaville still did not have a fire department, and citizens tried using blankets and buckets to fight the flames, but in the end, only rubble and embers remained of two entire blocks. Rebuilt of brick, the south side of the street never suffered another major fire, but the shops and saloons on the north side, which were quickly rebuilt from wood, were again destroyed on August 28, 1890, when someone set fire to Chapman's Harness and Saddlery Shop on the corner of Dobbins and Main Streets, and the winds again drove the fire all the way to the creek.

In 1892, the area around Vacaville, Dixon, and Winters was struck by a major earthquake, and while Vacaville suffered the least damage, most of the new brick structures had their facades tumbled into the street. The earthquake damage was repaired, and most of these buildings are still standing today.

Vacaville has grown rapidly since the 1940s, when the population was 1,608; the small village that sprang up to serve the early ranches and orchards of the 1850s is now a vibrant city. The south side of town had for years been separated by the heavy traffic along Highway 40 until construction began on a six-lane freeway along the southern edge of the city in 1961. With the new overpasses and freedom from the constraints of heavy traffic, the city soon saw residential growth to the south, along with supporting schools and retail centers. The addition of another freeway at the north end of town encouraged the development of business parks that are now home to medical centers, offices, warehouses, light manufacturing, and a growing life-science industry. As the population now approaches 100,000, an ever-expanding inventory of housing now occupies much of the former orchard and ranch land. In a cooperative effort with the neighboring town of Dixon, a greenbelt area was purchased that will serve as a buffer between the towns and a reminder of the agricultural heritage of the valleys.

The citizens of Vacaville are proud of their roots and have preserved much of their history through the adaptive reuse of the heritage buildings. A thriving downtown business district is located in buildings dating back to the late 1800s. In 1961, when the redevelopment agency proposed removal of some of the city's oldest buildings in the heart of the downtown, the community reacted by removing the city council and mandating an end to redevelopment. One of the buildings saved from destruction is the 1907 town hall, which is owned by the City of Vacaville and now serves as home to the Vacaville Heritage Council's archive of history and over 6,000 photographs, the Solano County Genealogy Society Library, and also the business offices of the Solano County Historical Society and the Peña Adobe Historical Society. The Vacaville Heritage Council Website at www.VacavilleHeritageCouncil.org lists many of the resources available; the photographic index includes the names of the families who have donated to our collections. We are currently seeking grants and donations to place our entire collection online for public access.

As the community celebrates the 100th anniversary of the dedication of "Old Town Hall" of July 18, 2007, it is with both pride and in some cases sadness that we look back at the changes that have taken place, to quote Richard Rico's column in the *Vacaville Reporter*, "since the time when everyone knew your name."

CHAPTER 1

MEMORIES

A favorite spot for picnics and parties in early Vacaville was Towson's Grove, located east of Pleasants Valley Road and north of Foothill Drive. This 1896 photograph shows the young ladies weaving the Maypole at the May Day picnic. Note how formally they are dressed to go on a picnic.

In 1883, F. B. Tucker erected Vacaville's first jail: a 10-foot-high wooden building measuring 12 feet by 16 feet in diameter was placed on the creek bank. One night, it is told, two inebriated occupants dismantled the jail, and after neatly stacking the wood, both went home. When the little jail was pushed down into the creek by vandals, plans were begun for a town hall. The trees that surround the Creekwalk Plaza now obscure the 20th-century view.

The entire student body of Vacaville High School, all four grades, are pictured in front of the cottage on Parker Street owned by Fred Chandler, which served as the high school for six years before the classes were moved to the second floor of the brick grammar school in 1896. The high school finally had its own home when George Sharpe completed the building in 1898. This site is now the parking lot of Teriyaki House directly behind the city's new transportation center.

Located on the northwest corner of Main and Dobbins Streets, Frank C. Chapman's Harness and Saddlery Shop was a busy place when this photograph was taken. In August 1890, an arson fire that started in the shop destroyed all the businesses and homes from Main Street north between Dobbins and the Ulatis Creek Bridge. The offices of Kappel and Kappel Realty are now located on this site.

The Rogers boys ride in their governess's pony cart past the Baptist church on School Street about 1900 in one of Vacaville's many parades. The unoccupied church building was removed in the early 1920s when the Ulatis School Auditorium was constructed on the northwest corner of McClellan Street. The school was torn down in 1953 when state safety inspectors ruled it was structurally unsafe. The steps and parts of the foundation walls of the auditorium remain.

The adobe erected by Juan Felipe Peña in 1842 stands as the centerpiece of Peña Adobe Park. Designated as a historic landmark in 1955, it was donated by William Goheen and the Phil Mowers family in 1959. Shown after it was sheathed in a wood frame to protect the adobe walls and add additional living space in the 1880s, the addition has now been set off to one side and serves as a small museum. Tours are available by appointment through the Peña Adobe Historical Society.

The first Oakdale School, shown, was built in 1885, and this photograph of the teacher and student body was taken in 1886. When a new schoolhouse was built in 1935, it was said to be the noted division point between the Pleasants and Vaca Valleys. Most rural district schools served a dual function, as classroom by day and at other times as the community meeting and social hall. When the last semester ended in 1960, the property was sold and the building renovated; today it is a beautifully maintained private residence.

Superintendent A. P. Sanborn's 1899 census report showed the Browns Valley district with 25 children between ages 5 and 17 and eight children under age 5. When the first class met at this new building in 1920, thirty students were enrolled in grades one through eight and all were taught in a single, large classroom. A new, year-round campus called Browns Valley was later built on Wrentham Drive. This building, once abandoned in ruins, is now a home, and once again children play in the yard.

In 1895, James Monroe Parker built Vacaville Steam Laundry at what was later given the address of 406 Merchant Street. He operated the business until 1898 when he sold to the Miyashita family who returned to Japan in the 1920s. Several other successful operators followed, and many people were employed. The Vacaville Steam Laundry truck pictured in 1925 serviced routes throughout the city. Demolished in 1949, another very successful family business, Pietro's Pizza, placed a building on the site in 1956 with an entry that faces Cernon Street.

The Vacaville Hotel was a welcome addition when it opened to much hoopla on Merchant Street near the corner of Mason Street in 1920; the town had been without a hotel since the Raleigh Hotel fire in 1909. In 1936, a fire claimed the two-story section of the hotel, and the Saturday Club took over the remainder as their meeting hall. Bank of America built there in 1956, relocating the Saturday Club to Kendal Street, and U.S. Bank has the current building on the site.

Nestora Lyon's Casa Maria Restaurant, on Merchant Street across from the Triangle Building, was named in honor of her mother, Maria Vaca Peña Lyon, a member of the founding family of Vacaville. She advertised dining and dancing under the trees in the open courtyard. To entice travelers along the Lincoln Highway in the 1930s, she offered lunch for 50¢, dinner for 75¢, fountain specialties, candies, and afternoon tea. Cheers Pub, Chancellor Graphics, and other small shops now occupy this space.

By 1902, one-third of the orchard land in the Vaca Valley was owned or rented by the Japanese, and those of the Buddhist faith made plans to build a temple. Dedicated November 13, 1912, the delightful structure was on the southwest corner of Monte Vista Avenue and Dobbins Street; a Japanese language school opened on the adjoining Dobbins Street lot in 1928. The temple was destroyed by fire in November 1951, but application has been made for a state historical marker on the site. Pearson's Florist is now located here.

Fire chief Warren Hughes finally got the new firehouse he wanted in 1957, when the volunteer firefighters contributed over 3,000 hours of labor and the community added another 500 man-hours. Until that time, the department had always had a place to store its equipment, but never a place to call home. As the city expanded, four new firehouses were built in other locations, and the John McBride Senior Center was built on the old firehouse site.

A hitching post can still be found in front of the house at 325 West Street. Aleen Burton, a longtime Vacaville resident, is shown greeting visitors at her gate. The square cement pillars with a large metal ring imbedded in the top for tying the reins can also be found on Cernon Street and other streets in that area.

Vacaville's first strip mall, in the 600 block of Merchant Street, was the location of the Lorenzo family's Vaca Valley Shopping Center and the McKenzie family's Pacific Ace Hardware, which still remains on the site as Solano County's favorite hardware store. Albert McKenzie started the business with a general store in the town of Monticello in 1893, and it was relocated to Vacaville in 1957 when Monticello was inundated with water by the dam that created Lake Berryessa.

The hundreds of Vacavillians who were born there lovingly refer to this small, Queen Anne cottage at 331 Elizabeth Street built in 1888 as "Dr. Jenney's Hospital." Built as a residence, it was converted to a maternity hospital and outpatient clinic by Ann Tillman for the use of Dr. Warren Jenney so his patients would no longer be required to go to Fairfield. The first baby, Vance Killingsworth, was delivered on June 13, 1932, and many more would follow until the state forced its closure in 1946. It is once again used as a residence.

CHAPTER 2

The Master Builders

This publicity piece from 1905 of the mansions along Buck Avenue clearly shows the artistic workmanship of the master builders of that time. Most of the homes are the work of master builder George Sharpe. Some of these homes can still be viewed today at 201 Buck Avenue, 212 Buck Avenue, 225 Buck Avenue, and 301 Buck Avenue.

In 1891, the Christian Church awarded a contract for $4,975 to George Sharpe for a new building on their property near the southeast corner of Catherine and Wilson Streets, to be completed in 90 days. During the Depression, George Sharpe repurchased the building, and it was dismantled, the redwood lumber being used to build homes in the area. Vacaville's oldest established church, the Christian Church of Vacaville, is now located at 66 Vine Street. Opportunity House, a shelter for homeless families, is currently located on the site but will be moving, as redevelopment of the entire area will begin shortly.

In 1898, George Sharpe erected the Vacaville High School, and in 1908, he demolished the 1885 brick grammar school building shown that was weakened in the 1892 earthquake, and he built a new school building on the same site. The schools stood as proud monuments on Andrews Park Hill for many years. A plaque and the bells from the two schools mark the location of the high school, and the school district offices are on the former grammar school site.

This magnificent residence of Sidney C. Walker once stood at 324 Catherine Street on the southwest corner of Davis Street near the Walker Opera House. Like many of Vacaville's large homes, it was converted to apartments to provide wartime housing. A fire that originated in one of the apartments severely damaged the house on November 13, 1959, and it was demolished. Today the site is occupied by a parking lot.

James Koford built this Victorian house at 118 Main Street in 1897 for Irene Moore for $1,300. George Gates purchased the home in 1903, and it remained in the family for three generations until 1977. The carriage house in the rear was once a two-story hay barn and stable. Still used as a residence, a 1977 addition doubled the size of the home, but the only visible change from the front is the alteration of the front porch.

The three-story Colonial Revival–style house at 306 Buck Avenue was one of several that George Sharpe built for himself only to later sell and build another. The 1896 home was sold to hardware merchant W. E. Lawrence in 1905; in 1914, Lawrence in turn sold to George P. Akerly, once a leading merchant in Vacaville, who later transferred the house to his son, George P. Akerly Jr. Today the exterior of the home appears exactly as it was constructed.

The home on the corner of Luzena and West Streets was moved from its prior location on the northeast corner Parker and Merchant Street in 1925 to make room for a service station at a time when Merchant Street was part of the Lincoln Highway to Sacramento. Purchased from a Mrs. Brown by Tina Mowers, it was converted to four apartments after the move. Beautifully restored, it is now appears to be a private residence once again.

Constructed some time before 1893, little is known of the origin of the house at 500 Davis Street, located outside the town limits. Built for a Mr. Blake, this was Ellen Phillips's boarding house in 1907. The landlady and her eight children catered mostly to the teachers from the nearby schools. Their special treat was fresh milk from the cow they kept pastured out back. In 1995, Nancy French purchased, restored, and remodeled it into 3,300 feet of commercial space.

In 1886, when W. W. Smith built his house and a barn, he selected a spot in a grove of trees against the foot of the hill north of Vaca Valley Road and east of Bucktown Lane. In 1879, he had 165 acres planted with 4,000 cherry trees. Later Dr. Irving W. Robbins purchased the ranch, and it became known as the Ulatis Ranch. Today nothing remains of the orchard and buildings.

Vacaville's first "speculation" developer was Meredith Miller, who purchased a square block bounded by Elizabeth, Stevenson, Mason, and Boyd Streets and, with his son James, who was the town's druggist, began home construction in 1884. Some of the oldest existing homes in Vacaville can still be seen in the 400 block of Elizabeth Street; many have now been adapted to commercial use.

Builder Will Hay is shown with his family in 1927 outside a row of houses he built on West Street between Luzena Avenue and Merchant Street. Later, when he grew tired of driving his daughters in from the country every day for school, he picked up his country house and moved it to town at 224 Stevenson Street. Hauling the house with a tractor, it took a week to move, during which time his wife and daughters continued to live in the house. This house at 206 Stevenson is a one of the many Craftsman-style homes he constructed in Vacaville.

A representative example of the new master builders is Holzapple Construction, whose restored office at 400 Cernon Street is pictured. The home is a wonderful example of the restoration work being done on the vintage housing stock surrounding the downtown area and out in the valleys.

3 CHAPTER

A Stroll Downtown

On the 100th anniversary of the dedication of Old Town Hall on July 17, 1907, stroll through historic downtown at a time when all merchants were located along Main Street and Buck Avenue was only two blocks long and called West Main Street. This 1908 postcard view shows Main Street looking west from Davis Street; notice the absence of automobiles. Noisy automobiles spooked the horses and were banned from town on weekdays, when the fruit-wagons were delivering their loads to the trains.

The southeast corner of East Main Street was for many years the location of George Akerly's first store, which opened in 1888. He sold everything from produce to hardware, most of it displayed on the wooden sidewalk outside the store. A large watering trough was out front for the country folk to water their horses. His motto was, "If you can't find it at Akerly's, there is no use looking further." The building was demolished in 1972, and this is now the location of the KUIC Radio Building.

The town was incorporated on August 9, 1892, for the second time, and occupied rented quarters until 1907, when Old Town Hall was erected. Town hall was the location of all the functions of the town: the constable, marshal, courthouse, jail, and storage for two hose carts, which were pulled by hand by the fire volunteers. It is said that when the bell tolled in the middle of the night, it could "wake the dead." The police department and parks and recreation department were the last city occupants, and town hall is now the home to Vacaville Heritage Council Archives and the Solano County Geological Society Library.

Things have changed considerably for law enforcement since Joe Stadtfeld was the only constable. He kept his horses out back in a stable on Davis Street and shared his office space with the Solano County marshal. In 2006, this new police headquarters building was dedicated as part of the city's office complex on Merchant Street.

On the corner of East Main and Wilson Streets, where Opportunity House now has their thrift store, was Al Bowle's large, tin, storage building that later was converted to a skating rink. Then came the fruit companies and loading docks. The train tracks were located four feet below street level so that the doors were level with the street and the wagons could back up to the doors. The cars were heavily insulated, and 100-pound blocks of ice were placed in bunkers at each end before the train departed and at stops along the way. St. Mary's Church on Catherine Street, which was destroyed by fire in 1925, is pictured in the background.

Across the creek on School Street was the old Ulatis Grammar School. This two-story brick building was damaged in the 1892 earthquake. By 1908, the building was so unstable that builder George Sharpe was hired to design and construct a new wooden building at the same location. Seen on the far left in this 1888 photograph is the old college building, which was replaced by the high school. The school district offices are now located at this site. Note the Lincoln Highway marker that is a reminder of when the highway to Sacramento ran through the heart of town.

In 1929, a brick combination gymnasium and classroom building was added in front of George Sharpe's 1898 high school on the corner of College and School Streets. The building stood until it was destroyed by fire on July 30, 1954, ending the city's hopes of converting the building for use as city hall. The school had already relocated its new campus. The Andrews Park Great Wonders Playground is located at the high point in the park, where the original high school building once stood.

A row of palm trees was planted in 1905 by Thomas Wilson, the son of Mason and Luzena Stanley, Wilson who were Vacaville's first hotel and restaurant proprietors. The Wilsons were the original owners of the School Street property and the surrounding area. Composed mostly of sandstone, holes had to be blasted in the creek bank before the 33 trees could be planted. Many of these trees still can be viewed along the creek.

County engineer Frank A. Steiger designed the Ulatis Creek Bridge, which today serves as the entrance to Carroll Plaza at the Creekwalk, in 1911. It replaced the old, wooden, horse-and-wagon bridge pictured, which had been almost washed away by the raging waters of the creek the year before. A Napa contractor named Gildersleeve built the reinforced concrete bridge for $7,870. With a span of 40 feet, it was 20 feet wide, separated by a railing from an additional 10 feet of walkway that was later combined with the road to allow two modern automobiles to pass. Shown is today's view of the bridge as viewed from the Creekside Bar and Grill patio.

Crossing the bridge, the first little shop was Polly Higgins's variety store, then came Nate Holt's cobbler shop, Grove's barbershop, and a saloon. The photograph shows the buildings as they would have been seen from Akerly's wagon as he prepared to make his deliveries. By the 1920s, these old wooden buildings had all been replaced. The Creekside Bar and Grill, with a patio below street level overlooking the creek, is now located here.

The Wells Fargo Express office with Richard Rammers as agent came next; their horse and wagon met all of the incoming and outgoing trains to pick up and deliver express packages. Wooden's Harness Shop next door made and repaired harness, buggy, and wagon equipment. Saltato's Restaurant and the Spin-A-Yarn shop are now located here.

Gonsalves Saloon had a vat in the rear filed with grapes where his many children would get in and stomp the grapes to make wine. The saloon building and Huey's Pub next door are the only structures remaining from the early 1900s; this one is now the location of the China House Restaurant.

In 1912, Vacaville Livery and Feed, which had been set back from the street, constructed a building to match the Killingsworth garage next door; it had an opening to their original barn in the rear. The Vacaville Garage, owned by Wiley Killingsworth, was on the corner of Bernard Street and had a center entrance. On one side of the entry was the garage, and Vacaville Water and Light Company was on the other. This is now the location of Town Square Plaza and Pure Grain Bakery.

The garage was the showroom for early automobiles, and Douglas Killingsworth taught the new car owners how to drive. He said some got confused, yelling "Whoa" to stop, forgetting the car was not their old horse. The Vacaville Garage had a side door on Bernard Street, and when the town purchased its first motorized fire truck, which was too large for Old Town Hall, it was parked inside this door ready for the volunteers to climb aboard when the bell sounded.

Across Bernard Street (now Town Square Plaza) a large tin building used as a dance hall was set back from the street. On Saturday night, a three-piece orchestra was brought in from San Francisco to play. In front was the Vacaville Band Stand, a small, round pavilion that stood about six feet off the ground; people would come early to get a good spot to park their wagon for the evening's concert. George Neal was the conductor and trumpet player for the band that was composed of local talent.

Hyde's Butcher Shop was the next building, and then the post office. Eliza Stitt was the postmistress, and Olive Foutz and R. R. Winters worked as her assistants. Everyone had his or her own post office box, as there was no home mail delivery service. Ed Miller's Ford Garage and Rudy Werner's Creamery later replaced the bandstand and these buildings. Los Reyes Restaurant is now located here.

Next was W. T. Sweeney's newspaper agency, which sold the Sacramento and San Francisco papers as well as bread and bakery goods that were brought in daily from the Bay Area. Sweeney's stepson, Elmer Thomas, delivered the papers around town. In the next office was Ralph Platt, who would later serve as judge in Vacaville. Los Reyes Restaurant and North Bay Hospice's thrift store now share this space.

The Masonic Temple occupied the upper floor of the Schroeder Building—another George Sharpe creation on the northeast corner of Main and Dobbins Streets—along with Dr. Jenney's office and Cecelia Clark's beauty shop. On the ground floor were the telephone company and the Schroeder and Frahm Hardware and Appliance Store, which later became Schroeder and Lawrence and then the location of Akerly's new store until it was destroyed in the fire that claimed the entire building in 1939. This is now the site of the North Bay Hospice's thrift store and parking lot.

At the opposite corner of Dobbins and Main Streets were Rachel Tucker's Millinery Shop and Tom Kowanda's Men's Tailoring Shop. J. A. Malone had a small store that carried a limited stock of groceries. Jessie Hay, who made all of her hats from scratch, had a very small shop next door. In the last small shop was the jewelry and watch repair business of H. J. Roach. Next was the mortuary operated by the Stewart family. This is now the location of the Chandler Building and Chandler Realty.

On the corner of Parker and Main Streets stood the Raleigh Hotel owned by Raleigh Barcar who also owned the *Vacaville Reporter*. Fire started in the wooden hotel on July 11, 1909, and embers ignited the steeple of the Presbyterian church across the street, now known as the Community Presbyterian Church. By the time the two-wheeled hose cart was pulled down the street, it was too late to save the hotel, but the firemen were able to pull the church steeple down with a rope and save the church. Once the location of the downtown post office, it is now the Old Post Office Seafood and Grill.

A new Presbyterian church was erected in 1892 to replace their former building that had burned, and the pastor's residence came next along Main Street. This marked the end of the business district, and the residential district continued out Main Street and two blocks along Buck Avenue (West Main Street) to the end of town.

Shown in this aerial photograph from 1962 is the block bounded by Main, Parker, Kendal, and Cernon Streets. All of the buildings have been razed, including the church and the pastor's home, which were removed shortly after the photograph was taken. Note the houses still located across Main Street. A new Safeway Store opened here for a while, and the building is now occupied by Gold's Gym.

This is a view down Parker Street from Main Street in 1888. The house on the right is on the southwest corner of Parker and was occupied by grocer Sterling Dobbins and his family in the early 1900s. The pole marks the location of the Carnegie Library; this was once the location of Vacaville's first downtown parking lot, with spaces to tie up rigs and wagons while doing the family shopping. Today's view is quite different.

Across Main Street, the Carnegie Library building is visible. Through the fund-raising efforts of the Saturday Club, the lot was purchased in 1914 for $3,000, and George Sharpe was awarded the building contract. It opened on July 17, 1915, was and lovingly referred to as "Ester's Library." George's daughter, Ester Eldredge, became the librarian in 1945 and remained until her retirement 20 years later. In 1970, the library was relocated to the new city complex on Merchant Street, and the building is now home to the chamber of commerce.

The theater site was also part of the wagon parking lot until July 1926, when W. J. Clark opened his theater. Designed for live performances and silent movies, it boosted a massive 600-pipe organ expressly designed for the theater and seating for 422 patrons. Jeweler Fred Deakin and another small shop used the first-floor interior. A ticket kiosk was a separate structure out front, and three sets of double doors admitted patrons. By 1930, "talkies" had become the main attraction, and a new screen and Vitaphone equipment were added. This was Vacaville's only theater for many years. The building is not currently used as a theater.

The next three buildings have a new facade added to make them appear as one building, but in the 1900s, the first two-story brick structure was the last of the business buildings on this side of the street and was home to Miss Gilles's Millinery Store on the ground floor, with living quarters and the osteopathic office of Dr. Jerome Wirt above. Bell Brothers Construction now occupies the building.

The following item was listed in the *Vacaville Reporter* on March 26, 1898: "Raleigh Barcar-two story brick, 50X80 on Main Street with two large (retail) store rooms on the first floor and five large office rooms and the Ulatis Club rooms above. Also a one-story brick 25X80, built expressly for the Reporter Office, total $9,500." Raleigh Barcar and Robert McMillan occupied a small law office to the left of the Reporter entrance. The Bella Terra shop is now located in the one-story section.

Evert Williams Ice Cream Parlor was next. Williams was the pianist for most hometown dances. Bert Deakin had a jewelry counter near the front entrance of the store. The other half of the building was occupied by William Godfrey's picture show, where silent movies were shown nightly. The fire department later occupied this space. The upper floor was living quarters and a lodge hall, which was also used for ballroom dancing. The Moose Lodge met here until moving to a new building on Gibson Canyon Road. The Handcrafters Gallery, Fatman Entertainment, and Kool Kids clothing shop now share the ground floor.

Sterling Dobbins Grocery Store was for groceries only. Patrons usually did not come to the store; they would telephone the shop with their orders in the morning, and one of the three Dobbins boys would take the horse and wagon to deliver them in the afternoon. Holly B's Bridal Boutique now occupies 344 Main Street.

The wagon on the right is located at corner of Main and Dobbins Streets, where this brick structure was built by the Crystal brothers in 1889 for their dry goods store, which became the largest in town. The building was fronted by an awning that overhung the boardwalk along unpaved Main Street. Above the picture windows was a transom area of leaded glass with cast-iron pilasters running the entire length of the facade. Now divided into separate shops, part of the building retains some of the original 12 pilasters. Amphlett's Interiors and the Main Street Salon are the current occupants.

The Triangle Building, also called the Hutton Block, was built in 1897 by Frederick Hutton and presented to his wife, Charlotte. The store frontage has been modernized with tile and stucco, but the original brickwork and arched windows and doorways are visible on the sides and rear. Elaborate cornice, dentil, frieze, and bay windows decorate the facade. The west end of the building was occupied by Schaffer's, an exclusive men's store. Ray's Cycle, a long-term tenant on the side of the building, now occupies the entire west end.

In 1911, the central portion of the Triangle Building was remodeled by George Sharpe for the First National Bank of Vacaville. The original vault remains in the basement from this remodel. James Miller's Drug Store, followed by Vacaville Drug Store, were the tenants in the east end of the building from 1903 until closing in 1991. The offices of Kappel and Kappel Mortgage are now located in the former drugstore space.

The corner of Merchant and Main Streets has two small buildings of note. The Heritage House Café is located near the site of the first merchandise store opened by E. F. Gillespie in 1854; it became an agent for Wells Fargo in 1857 and also was Vacaville's first post office. A commemorative monument records the location as the Pony Express stop in 1865. The events are reflected in a mural atop the store. For a while, the Lorenzo family used the building for their Star Bakery, and it is now the home of the popular Heritage House Café.

The 1897, two-story brick building at 307 Merchant Street, was home to Karl Kopp's Vienna Bakery in the 1900s; a horse and wagon delivered his goods. Later known as Star Bakery, it was purchased by Frank Lorenzo and his two cousins for $7,000. In 1938, the three partners bought out the California market, and in 1948, Frank sold his share and built a market called the Vaca Valley Shopping Center on Merchant Street in partnership with his children, which they operated until 1970. Eagle Eye Engraving is now located here. Also shown are the two statues commemorating the area's past connection to the fruit growing industry.

Crossing Merchant Street, 438 Main Street was built in 1902 by George Sharpe for Trent Hewitt on land his father, Samuel, had purchased from the Blums in 1897. The Hewitt Jewelry Store shared space with R. L. Reid Drug Store, just as they had done in their former location in the Walker Building. The drug store also had a soda fountain and was the postal telegraph office. This is now the office of State Farm Insurance.

The building at 444 Main Street was constructed as a meat market in 1902 on the site of one of Vacaville's first buildings that burned in the fire of 1888. Butch Akinson was the buyer and ran the slaughterhouse on Brown Street; Ceaser Pardi was the butcher and ran the shop. In 1940, the Lopez family moved Barber Joe's to this location and later remodeled it to include the shop on the corner, which had housed Gillespie Cleaners, and updated the facade. The original 1902 brickwork can be seen on the side and rear of the building.

On the corner was Goldman Department Store, later owned by the Glickbarg family. The Bank of Vacaville purchased this location in 1921 and erected the current building. The Bank of Italy bought them out in 1923, shortly after the building was completed, and later the name was changed to Bank of America. Judge Walter Weir occupied the building as his law offices when the bank relocated, and the law offices of Donald Stephenson now occupy the space.

Built in 1885 by S. C. Walker, this building was home to the J. and I. Blum Mercantile Store, among others. In 1910, Anita and Nestora Lyon used the building as a movie theater. Awnings and arches have been added to the updated facade, and Jackson Medical Supply now shares the space with the El Patron restaurant.

In November 1888, E. L. (Ray) Bennett replaced his wooden saloon with a new brick building after a fire destroyed most of the buildings along the south side of Main Street. The facade was decorated with stained-glass windows and inside displayed the finest wood paneling. Always sporting diamond shirt studs and rings, he put out the best free lunch to be found. The upper floor was used as living quarters. Used as a photographer's studio, much of the building's original charm is still apparent.

Constructed for McWilliams Grocery after the 1888 fire, 528 Main Street was later divided. Frank Deakin's Barber Shop, where one could get a 15¢ shave, a 25¢ bath, or a haircut, was in front, and Gus Maurer ran a cigar store and poolroom in the rear. The other half was Fred Bissel's Haberdashery and also the Western Union telegraph agent. The site was then a long succession of restaurants. The new owners hope to remove the stucco that now hides the original facade.

The I.O.O.F. Building at 534 and 536 Main Street proudly displays the date 1889 on the facade that was toppled in the 1892 earthquake. Quickly restored, it is a grand example of past architectural style. The lodge hall upstairs was a popular dance hall, as it had the only maple hardwood floor in town, and was used also by the Episcopal church until their building at Main and West Streets was completed. Down below, the saloon in the Burns Hotel, owned by Johnny Burns, also served a free lunch. The Mirage Salon and Spa occupies the ground floor, and the Independent Order of Odd Fellows still meets upstairs.

The Bank of Vacaville, where Ed Fisher was the cashier, occupied 542 Main Street from 1902 until 1921, when it relocated to its new office at the end of the block on the corner of Elizabeth Street. In 1890, Hacke's Hardware was located at 548 Main Street and later became the Winfield family hardware store. Built in 1897 as Arnold and Bugbees Hardware Store, George Arnold occupied 554 Main Street in the 1900s with a small mercantile. The old facades of all three are hidden beneath false fronts, but hints of the past can be viewed from the rear. Ryan Bates Photography now occupies the old bank building.

The Walker Opera House building at 560 Main Street held a grand concert on opening night on September 25, 1897, in an elegant, 600-seat theater. But opera was never a hit in Vacaville, and the building was used for picture and stage shows and high school dances. In half of the ground floor was Edstrom's Ice Cream Parlor and Candy Store, which offered curb-side service to the ladies seated comfortably in their own buggies. TJ s Lounge now occupies the Arnold and Bugbees location at 554 Main Street.

On the corner was a grocery store operated by Rolla Gray and the Grand Theater, and in the rear was the Ulatis, an exclusive men's club, which was entered through a door on Davis Street. The upper floor was unused for a long period of time before the Masonic Lodge took it over in 1939 after fire destroyed their building. Today Merchant and Main Catering use the upper floor for luncheons and special occasions.

CHAPTER 4

THE VALLEYS

Looking down from the Zimmerman Ranch in Upper Vaca Valley there are only orchards and fields as far as the eye can see; the few buildings that make up the town of Vacaville are visible in the upper right corner of the photograph. Today this view would be an orchard of houses rather than trees.

Many wagonloads of fruit were shipped from this packing shed, a part of the vast Bucktown fruit growing operations of Congressman Frank Buck until the summer it burned to the ground. The tall wagon loaded with baskets of peaches fresh from the orchards is driven be Ernie Laferriere in this 1914 photograph, and Frank Buck is standing in front of it in the white helmet. This barn on Bucktown Lane is the only one of the original buildings still to be seen among the orchards.

Edward R. Thurber purchased 168 acres of farmland along Pleasants Valley Road in 1858. A pioneer in the valley fruit industry in the 1890s, his ranch was one of the largest in the valley. A bridge designed by Solano County engineer Frank Steiger was built in 1907 crossing the creek on the road adjoining his property, which was dedicated on the 100th anniversary of its construction on April 29, 2007, in the name of Edward R. Thurber. The present owners have completely restored the original ranch house.

In 1884, Eliza (Elsie) Buckingham purchased a home and 400 acres of land in Lagoon Valley from Jose Demetrio Peña where she planted pears, figs, walnuts, and vines. The most successful female fruit rancher of her time, Buckingham made Lagunita Rancho her home until her death in 1915. In 1888, she acquired 1,000 acres in the Butcher Tract, naming the area Ariquipa Rancho. Subdividing half into smaller parcels and selling them at auction, she more than recovered the purchase price of the land. Only the line of trees, split by I-80, that once lined the road are visible today.

W. B. Davis, who settled on his ranch in 1853, was one of the first ranchers in the area to venture into fruit growing. He was also one of the founders of Vacaville's first bank, the Bank of Vacaville. His granddaughter Hellen Davis was a well-known celebrity harness racer and the first woman to win at the state fair in 1928. The ranch, located across Sacramento Road (East Monte Vista Avenue) from the Harbison ranch (where the Nut Tree is located), is now the location of the Vacaville Premium Outlets.

This photograph of a Mr. Peter's sheep crossing Browns Valley Road taken in the 1950s reflects an era when all of Browns Valley was ranch land. The current photograph gives only a hint of the development that has taken place, with the barrier marking the end of the sidewalk just beyond Vaca Valley Parkway, and hidden just over the hill are hundreds of new homes under construction.

CHAPTER 5

TRANSPORTATION

Pictured is the John Mix family out for a Sunday ride, perhaps leaving their ranch in Mix Canyon for Sunday church services in the late 1800s. Not everyone had the luxury of such a fine rig; many people came to town along the dusty road with the wagon and team that was used to work the ranch during the week.

In July 1868, the tracks of the California Pacific Railroad finally reached Vaca Station (near Elmira), providing a faster mode of transportation to the shipping ports of Vallejo. Soon the little Vaca Valley railroad was completed to the junction in Elmira, and its engine made daily trips with the harvests from Vacaville. In 1877, the line was reincorporated as the Vaca Valley and Clear Lake Railroad and the line extended to Madison. Dreams of completing the line to Mendocino County and its timber supply were never realized. In 1888, the line was taken over by Southern Pacific and extended to Rumsey. Today Depot Street is only a few blocks long, leading to today's mode of transportation—the freeway.

In May 1914, electric interurban service began between Vacaville and Suisun. With four trips daily, the trains stopped in the Portland Cement Company town called Cement, located off Peabody Road between Fairfield and Vacaville, enabling the workers to reside outside the company town. The hope of providing freight service, breaking the monopoly of the Southern Pacific and reducing freight rates, was never realized, as passengers generated 90 percent of their revenue. Struggling through several changes in ownership and unable to compete with the automobile, it stopped carrying passengers in 1926. The tracks ran along Davis Street, terminating near where the California Automobile Association and First Northern Bank now have their offices.

The Lincoln Highway, between San Francisco and Sacramento, was completed through Vacaville in 1912 and would shape the area for many years to come as restaurants, service stations, and auto courts sprung up to serve the travelers who came over the bridges on Cherry Glen and Butcher Roads and followed Merchant Street into the heart of town. Traffic was confused in the early days because of a lack of road signs, as reflected in this picture of a hand-painted sign and arrow to direct traffic down School Street and out of town. Today only bicycles and pedestrians travel this route.

There was not a street named Alamo when this new Interstate 80 overpass was built in 1961, but its construction would change Vacaville completely as development now expanded to the south side of town and up the hill on the north, with new shopping centers and service stations to serve all the new residents. The population of Vacaville, which had been about 10,000 in 1960, would nearly double in each of the next three decades until annual limits were placed on the number of permits issued for new housing units.

Growth also is evident along the eastern edge of town, as these photographs taken from the freeway overpass reveal. The 1961 photograph from the Allison overpass shows only open fields along the freeway, and the current photograph, taken looking back from the next overpass at Nut Tree Road, shows the tremendous growth that has taken place over the years.

Merchant Street seemed totally devoted to the automobile when a prankster from the Fiesta Days Committee hung "Bad Sam" from the stoplight at the corner of Elm Street in May 1973. Note the 35.9¢-per-gallon gasoline at the Gulf Station. What a difference.

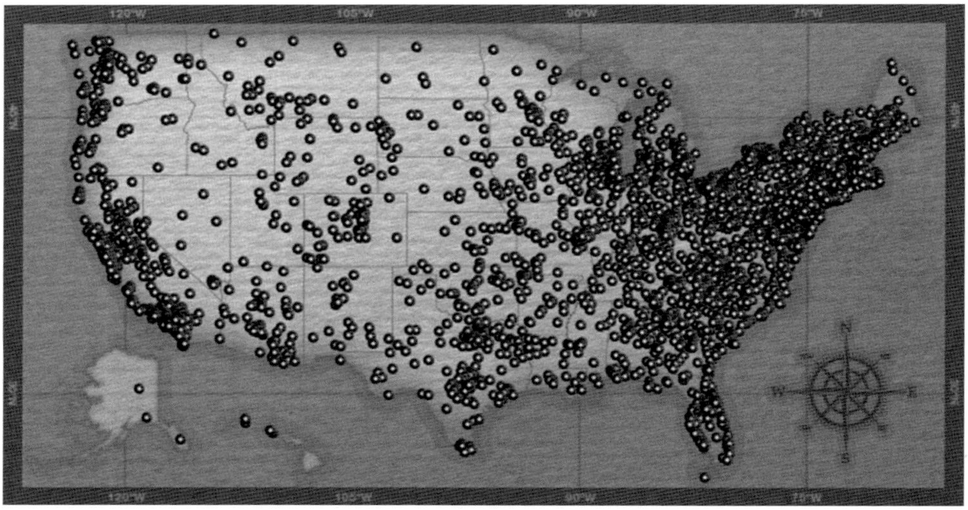

Consistent with our mission to preserve history on a local level, this book was printed in South Carolina on American-made paper and manufactured entirely in the United States. Products carrying the accredited Forest Stewardship Council (FSC) label are printed on 100 percent FSC-certified paper.

MADE IN THE USA